Autoethnography and Fen
Water's Edge

Sonja Boon • Lesley Butler • Daze Jefferies

Autoethnography and Feminist Theory at the Water's Edge

Unsettled Islands

palgrave
macmillan

Sonja Boon
Memorial University of Newfoundland
St John's, Canada

Lesley Butler
Memorial University of Newfoundland
St John's, Canada

Daze Jefferies
Memorial University of Newfoundland
St John's, Canada

ISBN 978-3-030-08109-6   ISBN 978-3-319-90829-8   (eBook)
https://doi.org/10.1007/978-3-319-90829-8

This Palgrave Pivot imprint is published by the registered company Springer International
Publishing AG part of Springer Nature.
The registered company address is: Gewerbestrasse 11, 6330 Cham, Switzerland

ACKNOWLEDGEMENTS

This book would not have been possible without the commitment and intellectual generosity of many. Our thanks to Sarah Boon for conversations about mud and geography; Karyn and Charlie Butler, for always offering Lesley an encouraging and attentive ear; Deirdre Connolly for her editorial assistance; Courtland Dearing and Violet Drake for sharing with Daze their continuous love and reassurance; Vicki Hallett for creative and decolonial insights about ice and for her graduate seminar on life writing; and Carol Lynne D'Arcangelis, Max Liboiron, Beth Pentney, Gina Snooks, Jocelyn Thorpe, and Mimi Yahn for well-placed reading suggestions. Deepest gratitude to the many cohorts of graduate students with whom Sonja has shared lively, passionate, and always critically engaged conversations about feminist theory. We also want to thank the three reviewers, whose comments and enthusiasm buoyed and motivated us, and Amelia Derkatsch at Palgrave, for her interest in—and support of—this project, right from the very beginning.

The beginning of this book finds its home in a collaborative research blog begun in 2015 within the context of a larger research project on memories, migrations, transnational histories, and complicated belongings funded by an Insight Development Grant from the Social Sciences and Humanities Research Council of Canada. Just under half the essays in this collection germinated there, hints of ideas that slowly took shape in the thinking and writing that ultimately became this book. As a way of acknowledging the generative impulse of blogs, with their windows into different modes of thinking, seeing, and being, we've created a website to accompany this book: unsettledislands.wordpress.com includes a range of pedagogical tools, from classroom prompts and activities, to photographs, and additional literature. While unsettledislands.wordpress.com is designed to complement the ideas presented in the book, it is separate from and not part of it, and is not managed by Palgrave.

Elements of some of these essays have been presented at conferences, symposia, and public events in both Canada and abroad. Thanks to those who engaged with this work at Talking Bodies (University of Chester, 2017), Creative Histories (University of Bristol, 2017), National Women's Studies Association (Montreal, 2016), Silenced Voices (St. John's, 2018), Women's and Gender Studies et Recherches Féministes (Calgary, 2016), International Small Island Cultures Conference (St. John's, 2017), the Nexus Centre Colloquium Series (St. John's, 2017), and Changing Political Landscapes (St. John's, 2018).

CONTENTS

CHAPTER 1

Introduction: Islands of the Imagination

Abstract This chapter situates islands as metaphorical spaces of the imagination and as epistemological openings. In particular, it argues that islands, islanders, and islandness offer unique perspectives through which to engage with theory making. Indeed, to live and think from an island is to think from a threshold space, a borderland between land and sea. More specifically, this chapter suggests that the water's edge—that unsettled boundary between the solid and the liquid—is a potent site of theoretical possibility, potential, and dreaming.

Keywords Islands • Islandness • Theory • Autoethnography • Newfoundland • Borderlands

The wind lashes around my body, ice drops flashing against my skin. Visibility nil, the weather report said, but still I am here. At the water's edge. Scanning the invisible horizon. Newfoundland, this island I have now called home for ten years, marks its presence in my every move, and islandness now seeps through all of my pores. Islandness has become central to who I understand myself to be. Leaving here cannot be accomplished by foot or by bike or by car. It means navigating an expanse of water that freezes over in the winter, or flying in windy and foggy skies that sometimes close—for days on end—to air traffic. Islandness means waking to the lonely call of the foghorn and watching icebergs glide

© The Author(s) 2018
S. Boon et al., *Autoethnography and Feminist Theory at the Water's Edge*, https://doi.org/10.1007/978-3-319-90829-8_1

silently by, their stately masses keeping coastal communities cool, sometimes until late in June. To live on an island is to orient oneself to an infinite horizon, to the sound of beach stones constantly rolling against one another, and to the sticky tanginess of saltwater between my toes. The ocean knows…

Islands, as many have observed, are mythical spaces located "somewhere … between the real and the unreal" (Zilmer 2012, 34). As sites of infinite possibility, islands are places "away" where anything can happen; they are environments of the imagination. For Charles Darwin, islands were uniquely controlled environments and thus ideal laboratories (Walker and Bellingham 2011, 7), a quality they still retain to this day (Hay 2006, 19). Is it any wonder, then, that utopias are often situated on islands?

I haven't always been an islander. For a long time, water did not flood my thoughts, my dreams, my bodily being. I spent much of my childhood on the prairies; for eleven years my identity was shaped by a low horizon that split gold from blue, wheat from sky. But just as wheat fields and prairie grasses undulate, so too does the ocean undulate. And just as the prairie stretches into eternity, so does the ocean promise an endless horizon. Perhaps, then, this islandness was already inside me, somewhere. But unlike the solid prairie earth, the ocean is always moving. Heaving. Rushing. Dancing. Rocking. And it is this constant motion that was so very disconcerting in the early days.

There are approximately 680 billion islands in the world (Ronström 2009, 171). Ten percent of the world's population lives on islands (Baldacchino 2007, 1), and roughly a quarter of UN member nations are island nations (Chamberlin 2013, x). These numbers reveal not only the importance of islands within the context of a globe organized around continents, but also the continued conceptual relevance of islands in the human imagination.

At its simplest, an island is a "thing in water" (Zilmer 2012, 10). Islands are defined not by the earth—as continents are—but by something much more volatile: water. In places like Newfoundland, the ocean is a capricious, powerful, unruly, and uncontrollable border whose moods fundamentally shape the idea of the island. Indeed, the edge, that point of tension between solid and liquid, land and water, is fundamental to understanding islands and islandness. As Pete Hay observes, "islanders are more aware of and more confronted by the fact of boundaries than are most peoples" (2006, 21).

As liminal spaces, islands serve as "a master metaphor" (Gillis, qtd. in Perera 2009, 21). Indeed, in the words of J. Edward Chamberlin, "[m] aybe stories themselves began with islands" (2013, xii). We might consider here, the mythical Muskoka island envisioned by L. M. Montgomery in her single adult novel, *The Blue Castle* (1926). Here the metaphorical castle—actually a ramshackle cabin—rises from the mists, a space outside of time where anything, seemingly, is possible, and where the heroine's long cherished but almost dashed dreams can come true. So, too, can we turn our eyes to L. M. Montgomery's fabled childhood home, Prince Edward Island, whose rolling green hills and red sands have provoked the romantic dreams of many a schoolgirl, and served as the backdrop for Japanese—islanders themselves—tourist cards and wedding photos. Further afield, we can consider Dionne Brand's Trinidadian island imaginary, as evoked in her 2001 work, *A map to the Door of No Return: Notes to belonging* (2001). Water shapes Brand's memory, dreams, and history.

But if islands have been imagined as magical places, they're also understood as dangerous: "Paradises, but also Gulags, are generally islands," writes Godfrey Baldacchino (2005, 248). As H.W. Menard observes, islands—even as mere possibilities—have been deeply threatening to explorers (1986, 6). Isolated and remote, islands can be prisons for marooned communities incapable of escape. We might think here not only of such literal prison islands as Tasmania or Alcatraz, but also of the dystopian island space evoked in William Golding's *Lord of the Flies* (1954), which examines the darkest underbellies of human social relations. We might even, perhaps, recall Daniel Defoe's Robinson Crusoe, who finds himself deposited on a Caribbean island, where he remains for twenty-eight years, forced to rely on his own resources: ingenuity, wit, education, and—tellingly—the support of a servile sidekick, a Carib man he names Friday, for his survival (Defoe 1719). This island space is not necessarily romantic; rather it tests resilience and the human will to survive.

"Every nation has its sacred isle, full of portent," writes Elizabeth Waterston, before going on to discuss Manhattan and Ellis Island in the USA and then Vancouver Island, Prince Edward Island, and Cape Breton Island in Canada (2000, 266). Surprisingly, here, Waterston appears to have forgotten Newfoundland, a darker and larger island to Prince Edward Island's immediate northeast. In contrast to the genteel character of Vancouver Island and Prince Edward Island, Newfoundland stands stark and wild. Windy and untamed, this rock faces the North Atlantic head on, subject fully to the whims of an unruly ocean. No rolling hills here, no gentle children's romances; instead, Newfoundland, as an island of the imagination, is a place hewn from rock, will, hard work, and determination. Newfoundland is not a romantic idyll; it is something else entirely.

I arrived in Newfoundland late in June 2008. June is peak fog season in St. John's, the province's capital and only real city, but as a Mainlander—a Come From Away—I didn't know this yet. Exhausted after twelve hours in transit from Vancouver, we found ourselves circling the airport for twenty minutes as the pilot waited desperately for the fog to lift just enough for us to land. Later, we would discover that our flight was the last to land for four days.

Weather. Water. Rock. Wind. There was much I didn't yet know about this place I was going to call home. I'd lived on three continents, in five countries, and five Canadian provinces before arriving on these shores. I knew what it meant to be a newcomer, knew the stages of transition. But what Newfoundland has offered me is something different from anything else I've experienced. Somewhere along these barren cliffs, among the rushing seas, between the haphazardly placed clapboard houses, Newfoundland started asking me to think about place, about identity, about bodies, about language, and about belonging.

Islands have multiple meanings. While Newfoundland has been imagined as a lonely place, an "isolated [outpost] adrift in a vast sea" (Ellis 2000, 52), other island groupings are almost intimate in character, their collective nature offering a glimpse into vital collaboration and exchange. Such island groupings inspire networked identities, a spatiality premised on shared experiences rather than on individuality and insularity (Ellis 2000, 52). But even Newfoundland's legendary—indeed, mythic—isolation can be reimagined. In a transportation imaginary organized by landscapes and roads, Newfoundland does indeed appear remote, an outpost far removed from 'civilization.' But in a world of seascapes and waterways, the island changes. Communities rendered virtually inaccessible by land are just a quick jaunt across a bay. Even Europe beckons, as the possibly apocryphal story of the outport fisherman who took his aging parents from Newfoundland's Burin Peninsula to Portugal to get their photos taken—a tale shared with me by a local folklorist—suggests. Island cultures are, by necessity, connected cultures profoundly reliant on goodwill and generosity within communities and on larger trade networks in order to ensure their long-term sustainability and viability (Hay 2006; see also Bjarnason 2010).

Newfoundland is a place of tangled histories, stories, and myths. It is a place of hauntings and mysteries. Settler Newfoundlanders cleave to their imagined histories, forging their identities with and through land and sea, in and through the weather (Manning 2017; see also Crummey 2009, 2014; Morgan 1992). Newfoundland's Indigenous histories, meanwhile, reach back thousands of years (see, for example, Marshall 1996; Martijn 2003; Neis 1995). Belonging locates itself deep within the body here, but that body is not a self-contained thing; rather, it must be understood as part and parcel of a larger web that includes land, sea, wind, language, history, and more. Identity is not just about culture here. It's not only about history, language, song, and story. It's about one's complete embeddedness in a wild, windy, untameable landscape and a heaving, unpredictable ocean. To be an islander is to make theory at the water's edge, where land and ocean meet.

Islands are good to think with. To live on an island, to think from an island, is to think from a threshold space, a borderland between land and sea. Indeed, the shoreline can be understood as a liminal space of potential and possibility (Hay 2006, 22). Anything can happen at the island's edge. It is this generative and imaginative impulse—experienced at the point of encounter between the critical and the creative—that informs our work here. In this series of essays, we understand islands and islandness as epistemological openings, sites from which to make and live theory. We locate ourselves at the shore. In the face of an endless horizon, we live and think from the water's edge.

What does it mean to make theory through self and place? What might an embodied approach to theory-making look like? At a conceptual level, we draw on the work of feminist, queer, trans, Black, and Indigenous thinkers and scholars working in a variety of disciplines, from geography and anthropology, to history, folklore, literature, visual arts, and gender studies. These include, but are not limited to: Sara Ahmed, Gloria Anzaldúa, Hélène Cixous, Vicki Kirby, Katherine McKittrick, Viviane Namaste, Astrida Neimanis, Christina Sharpe, Leanne Betasamosake Simpson, Jackie Stacey, Susan Stryker, Eve Tuck, and others. We also draw considerable inspiration from essayists, novelists, poets, and memoirists, among them Dionne Brand, M. NourbeSe Philip, and Fred Wah, creative thinkers and writers who make theory through their critical engagement with the imagination.

These scholars, writers, and thinkers have one thing in common: they are intrigued by the interstices, the margins, the spaces between, the borderlands.

Central to all of this thought is the interwoven nature of social, environmental, and political relations, the entangled—and, to draw on the work of Suparna Bhaskaran (2004), "curdled"—identities shaped by both human processes and natural environments. Anzaldúa (2012), for example, writes provocatively about the possibility of a *mestiza* consciousness, a consciousness founded upon ribbons of contested territories, where notions of belonging are troubled by the making and unmaking of borders and boundaries. In her work, Anzaldúa unites the social and cultural with the natural and the built, evoking a complex positioning shaped by sexuality, gender, and race on the one hand, and by place, space, language, and environment on the other. Equally influential is the boundary-crossing work of Cixous (Cixous and Calle-Gruber 1997), who sifts her family's ethnic and religious histories not only through Europe's ever-shifting national boundaries, but also across the landscape of French colonial spaces. Cixous' *entredeux* (Cixous and Calle-Gruber 1997), the point at which meaning collapses, has also been critical to our understanding of space, place, and identity.

But even as Anzaldúa and Cixous propose identity as a fluid border space shaped by continued fluxes and flows, their conceptual frameworks are founded on land, on a notion of place as a solid, material entity. By contrast, our approach—focused as it is on the water's edge—has, by necessity, been shaped by the conceptual potential of the contact zone (Pratt 2002); that is, by a lens that acknowledges the shore as a liminal space between the solid and the liquid—the land and the sea—as a space of encounter. In this, we are indebted to the work of thinkers like Astrida Neimanis (2012, 2013, 2017a, b, see also Chen et al. 2013), Suvendrini Perera (2009), Deborah Bird Rose (2007), and Christina Sharpe (2016), all of whom interrogate the conceptual potential of water, the ocean, and the shoreline.

The work of feminist posthumanist scholars, finally, has allowed us to bring questions of transcorporeality (Alaimo 2008), entanglement (Barad 2007), and assemblage (Bennett 2010) into our understandings of subjectivity and identity. If "we are all water," as Astrida Neimanis (2012, 2013) suggests, then what might it mean to locate ourselves at the borders between solid and liquid, at the shore that marks the point where water and land meet? What might it mean to situate ourselves within a larger ecosystem, where identity and belonging are shaped not only by human relations, but also by our encounters and engagements with the more-than-human world?

"Island meanings," writes Pete Hay, "...emerge from a deeply visceral lived experience. They are phenomenologically generated and articulated" (2006, 33). As such it stands to reason that we locate our work within the very flesh of our embodied selves. Such an approach also resonates with our locatedness as feminist scholars. In our essays, we weave autobiography with theory, crafting intimate, vulnerable, and critical reflection pieces in order to interrogate the possibilities, potentials and limitations of making theory at the water's edge.

Making theory from the self requires a critical engagement with autoethnography. In autoethnography, the researcher is the central research instrument (Ellis 1999, 2003, 2013; Islam 2008; Muncey 2010; Reed-Danahay 1997; Spry 2001, 2011). As Tami Spry observes, "the researcher is the epistemological and ontological nexus upon which the research process turns" (2001, 711). As a research methodology, autoethnography brings autobiographical experience and theory together in order to interrogate and elucidate broader social processes (Boon 2012, 2017; Butz and Besio 2009; Chang 2008; Denzin 2014; Ellis 1999, 2003; Ellis and Bochner 1996, 2000; Holman-Jones 2002; Muncey 2010; Snooks and Boon 2017; Spry 2001, 2009; Tsalach 2013; Tye 2010).

More recently, scholars have begun working collaboratively, considering how it is that narratives of self tangle through—and butt up against—one another, creating new meanings in the process (Alexander et al. 2012; Chang et al. 2013; Diversi and Moreira 2016; Holman-Jones et al. 2013; Snooks and Boon 2017; Spry 2016; Tuck and Ree 2013). Chang et al. liken this to a form of ensemble performance: while each individual instrument has its own voice, "the combination of multiple voices to interrogate a social phenomenon creates a unique synergy and harmony that autoethnographers cannot attain in isolation" (2013, 24). It is this synergy that we have sought to harness in our work.

In this collaborative venture, we operate from the premise of embodied autoethnography, concerned both with the embodied nature of political, social, and cultural relations (that is, how we are intersectionally shaped by our fleshy, material selves), and with the conceptual insights and knowledges that emanate from our lived experiences of our bodies (Blinne 2012; Boon 2012, 2017; Lau 2002; Spry 2009, 2011).

Our autoethnographic landscape includes elements of what Sidonie Smith and Julia Watson refer to as "everyday autobiography" (1996, 2): photographs, documents, memories, and observations. It is equally informed by the physical land- and seascapes of Newfoundland, this island that we—as scholars, thinkers, and writers—call home. Our geographies are deeply embodied; woven into both our thinking and our being, they also inform the theory that we produce.

Writing in 1929, Virginia Woolf argued that:

The book has somehow to be adapted to the body, and at a venture one would say that women's books should be shorter, more concentrated, than those of men, and framed so that they do not need long hours of steady and uninterrupted work. For interruptions there will always be. (Woolf 1988, 74)

For Woolf, the realities of women's lives did not lend themselves to the form of men's writing. If it is true, as Woolf suggests, that a book should be adapted to a body, then what form might a book authored by island bodies take? What might such a book feel like, look like, sound like?

In this book, our thinking and being have been shaped by the land- and seascapes of the island of Newfoundland. *Autoethnography and feminist theory at the water's edge: Unsettled islands* is a series of self-contained but thematically-linked micro-essays organized around four main themes: origins, geographies, language, and longings. This format—a series of micro-essays organized around shared themes—mirrors the geography of the place from which we write: rock, ocean, waves, and islands.

The shores of this island we call home are covered in beach stones, their rough edges worn smooth by the constant tumbling of the ocean currents. When they are wet, each one is a jewel, glowing rich and warm in the summer sun. As a group, they move and shift, telling stories of the ocean's roaring and raging. But in their constant tumbling, they tell each other's stories, too, shaping and polishing that warm smoothness that we cup in our hands.

The coves of this island have been carved by the endless roar of an always living ocean. In stormy weather, the ocean heaves and thrusts, its raw power flooding inlets. But in the warmth of a summer sun, the sea can be docile, calm, and sleek, its roar replaced by a gentle purr. The ocean is a volatile spirit; unruly and disruptive, sensual and seductive, its energy cannot be contained. Each wave tells a story; each one is a soundscape to a horizon.

So, too, can we imagine our essays in the form of an archipelago of the islands that make up the larger place called Newfoundland, among them Fogo, Ramea, Change Islands, Bell Island, New World Island, Twillingate Island, Little Bay Islands, Fox Island, Greenspond, and Newfoundland itself. In centuries past, many of these islands were inhabited; over time they've been abandoned, leaving cemeteries, concrete foundations, the leaning remnants of saltbox houses, and beneath them, the material traces of long Indigenous histories. Each island creates its own mainlands; radiating in and through the other, none makes sense without its counterparts. What does Fogo Island mean without the jagged bulk of Newfoundland, or Change Islands without its larger cousin, Fogo? And what do all of these islands, taken together, mean in relation to the larger mainland known as Canada? And yet, each of these island spaces is unique; each place populated by different personalities, subtly different histories, and different ways of thinking and being.

Islandness, as we imagine it, does not lend itself to long, expository writing. Islandness is fragmented, in constant motion, its energies diffused along the hundreds of tiny coves along its shores. Islandness is a series of archipelagos, the heaving of a stormy ocean, the docility of a summer sea at dawn. Islandness is the rattle of beach stones rolling with the surf, their edges worn smooth from their constant tumbling, their weight a reminder of the history of this place, their tinkling a resonance of the long journeys that brought them to these shores. It is the wind that rushes along the cliffs, tearing at our trees and howling between our houses, at other times a gentle caress, a warm embrace, reminding us that nothing is ever completely still here. And so our writing, too, is fragmented, mobile, multiple. Our ideas tumble and tangle; they heave and they seduce.

At a practical level, micro-essays enable us to examine various facets of different theoretical concepts in bite-sized, intimate, critical, and engaged readings. But so too, do they offer the possibility for unconventional reading. While readers can still read from start to finish, they are no longer tied to a linear approach. Indeed, our structure offers multiple points of entry and, from there, multiple possible directions. Some may prefer to forage through the text, a voracious berry-picking approach of sampling, picking, and choosing among the various essays as their interests direct them. Others, meanwhile, will stop and savour, enjoying the view before moving on. None, however, will be unmoved by their reading journeys. Indeed, as Mi'kmaq writer Shannon Webb-Campbell observes in a recent essay, "The Atlantic changes you. It's tough love, but there's nothing like it" (2017, n.p.).

Sonja Boon, St. John's, 2018

References

Alaimo, Stacy. 2008. Trans-corporeal feminisms and the ethical space of nature. In *Material feminisms*, ed. Stacy Alaimo and Susan Hekman, 237–264. Bloomington and Indianapolis: Indiana University Press.

Alexander, Bryant Keith, Claudio Moreira, and hari stephen kumar. 2012. Resisting (resistance) stories: A tri-autoethnographic exploration of father narratives across shades of difference. *Qualitative Inquiry* 18 (2): 121–133. https://doi.org/10.1177/1077800411429087.

Anzaldúa, Gloria. 2012. *Borderlands/La frontera: The new mestiza*. 4th ed. San Francisco: Aunt Lute Books.

Baldacchino, Godfrey. 2005. Islands—Objects of representation. *Geografiska Annaler* 87B (4): 247–251.

———, ed. 2007. *A world of Islands: An Island studies reader*. Charlottetown: Institute for Island Studies.

Barad, Karen. 2007. *Meeting the universe halfway: Quantum physics and the entanglement of matter and meaning*. Durham: Duke University Press.

Bennett, Jane. 2010. *Vibrant matter: A political ecology of things*. Durham: Duke University Press.

Bhaskaran, Suparna. 2004. *Made in India: Decolonizations, queer sexualities, trans/national projects*. Houndmills: Palgrave Macmillan.

Bjarnason, David. 2010. Island connections: Icelandic spatiality in the wake of worldly linkages. *Island Studies Journal* 5 (2): 217–236.

Blinne, Kristen C. 2012. Auto(erotic)ethnography. *Sexualities* 15 (8): 953–977.

Boon, Sonja. 2012. Autobiography by numbers; or, embodying maternal grief. *Life Writing* 19 (2): 191–202.

———. 2017. Dusting for fingerprints: Bodily traces, embodied memories and the forensic self. *Life Writing* 14 (1): 69–82. https://doi.org/10.1080/1448452 8.2016.1241207.

Brand, Dionne. 2001. *A map to the Door of No Return: Notes to belonging*. Toronto: Vintage Canada.

Butz, David, and Kathryn Besio. 2009. Autoethnography. *Geography Compass* 3 (5): 1660–1674. https://doi.org/10.1111/j.1749-8198.2009.00279.x.

Chamberlin, J. Edward. 2013. *Island: How islands transform the world*. Katonah: Blue Bridge.

Chang, Heewon. 2008. *Autoethnography as method*. Walnut Creek: Left Coast Press.

Chang, Heewon, Faith Wambura Ngunjiri, and Kathy-Ann C. Hernandez. 2013. *Collaborative autoethnography*. Walnut Creek: Left Coast Press.

Chen, Cecilia, Janine MacLeod, and Astrida Neimanis, eds. 2013. *Thinking with water*. Montreal: McGill-Queen's University Press.

Cixous, Hélène, and Mireille Calle-Gruber. 1997. *Hélène Cixous, Rootprints: Memory and life writing*. Trans. Eric Prenowitz. London and New York: Routledge.

Crummey, Michael. 2009. *Galore*. Toronto: Doubleday Canada.

———. 2014. *Sweetland*. Toronto: Doubleday Canada.

Defoe, Daniel. 1719. *The life and strange surprising adventures of Robinson Crusoe of York, mariner*. London: Taylor.

Denzin, Norman K. 2014. *Interpretive autoethnography*. 2nd ed. Los Angeles: SAGE.

Diversi, Marcelo, and Claudio Moreira. 2016. Performing betweener autoethno graphies against persistent us/them essentializing: Leaning on a Freirean peda gogy of hope. *Qualitative Inquiry* 22 (7): 581–587. https://doi. org/10.1177/1077800415617208.

Ellis, Carolyn. 1999. Heartful autoethnography. *Qualitative Health Research* 9 (5): 669–683.

Ellis, Juniper. 2000. Literary cartographies in Oceania. In *Message in a bottle: The literature of small islands*, ed. Laurie Brinklow, Frank Ledwell, and Jane Ledwell, 51–64. Charlottetown: Institute for Island Studies.

Ellis, Carolyn. 2003. *The ethnographic I: A methodological novel about autoethnography.* Walnut Creek: Altamira.

———. 2013. Crossing the rabbit hole: Autoethnographic life review. *Qualitative Inquiry* 19 (1): 35–45. https://doi.org/10.1177/1077800412462981.

Ellis, Carolyn, and Arthur P. Bochner, eds. 1996. *Composing ethnography: Alternative forms of qualitative writing.* Walnut Creek: AltaMira.

———. 2000. Autoethnography, personal narrative, reflexivity: Researcher as sub ject. In *Handbook of qualitative research*, ed. Norman K. Denzin and Yvonna S. Lincoln, 2nd ed., 733–768. Thousand Oaks: SAGE.

Golding, William. 1954. *Lord of the flies*. London: Faber and Faber.

Hay, Pete. 2006. A phenomenology of islands. *Island Studies Journal* 1 (1): 19–42.

Holman-Jones, Stacy. 2002. The way we were, are, and might be: Torch singing as autoethnography. In *Ethnographically speaking: Autoethnography, literature, and aesthetics*, ed. Arthur P. Bochner and Carolyn Ellis, 44–56. Walnut Creek: Altamira.

Holman-Jones, Stacy, Tony E. Adams, and Carolyn Ellis, eds. 2013. *Handbook of autoethnography.* Walnut Creek: Left Coast Press.

Islam, Naheed. 2008. Research as an act of betrayal: Researching race in an Asian community in Los Angeles. In *Just methods: An interdisciplinary feminist reader*, ed. Alison M. Jaggar, 471–483. Boulder: Paradigm Publishers.

Lau, Kimberly J. 2002. This text which is not one: Dialectics of self and culture in experimental autoethnography. *Journal of Folklore Research* 39 (2/3): 243–259.

Manning, Susan M. 2017. Contrasting colonisations: (Re)storying Newfoundland/ Ktaqmkuk as place. *Settler Colonial Studies*. Online First. https://doi.org/10. 1080/2201473X.2017.1327010.

Marshall, Ingeborg. 1996. *A history and ethnography of the Beothuk.* Montreal and Kingston: McGill-Queen's University Press.

Martijn, Charles A. 2003. Early Mi'kmaq presence in Southern Newfoundland: An ethnohistorical perspective, c. 1500–1763. *Newfoundland Studies* 19 (1): 44–102.

Menard, H.W. 1986. *Islands.* New York: Scientific American Books.

Montgomery, L.M. 1926. *The blue castle.* Toronto: McClelland and Stewart; New York: Frederick A. Stokes.

Morgan, Bernice. 1992. *Random passage*. Breakwater: St. John's.

Muncey, Tessa. 2010. *Creating autoethnographies*. Thousand Oaks: SAGE.

Neimanis, Astrida. 2012. Hydrofeminism: Or, on becoming a body of water. In *Undutiful daughters: New directions in feminist thought and practice*, ed. H. Gunkel, C. Nigianni, and F. Soderback, 85–99. New York: Palgrave Macmillan.

———. 2013. Feminist subjectivity, watered. *Feminist Review* 103: 23–31.

———. 2017a. *Bodies of water: Posthuman feminist phenomenology*. London: Bloomsbury Academic.

———. 2017b. Water and knowledge. In *Downstream: Reimagining water*, ed. D. Christian and R. Wong, 51–68. Waterloo: Wilfrid Laurier University Press.

Neis, Barb. 1995. A collage within a collage: Original traces of First Nations women. In *Their lives and times: Women in Newfoundland and Labrador*, ed. Carmelita McGrath, Barb Neis, and Marilyn Porter, 1–17. St. John's: Killick Press.

Perera, Suvendrini. 2009. *Australia and the insular imagination: Beaches, borders, boats, and bodies*. New York: Palgrave Macmillan.

Pratt, Mary Louise. 2002. The arts of the contact zone. In *Ways of reading: An anthology for writers*, ed. David Bartholomae and Anthony Petrosky, 604–662. Boston: Bedford-St. Martin's.

Reed-Danahay, Deborah, ed. 1997. *Auto/ethnography: Rewriting the self and the social*. Oxford: Berg.

Ronström, Owe. 2009. Island words, island worlds: The origins and meanings of words for 'islands' in North-West Europe. *Island Studies Journal* 4 (2): 163–182.

Rose, Deborah Bird. 2007. Justice and longing. In *Fresh water: New perspectives on water in Australia*, ed. Emily Potter, Alison Mackinnon, Stephen McKenzie, and Jennifer McKay, 8–20. Melbourne: Melbourne University Publishing.

Sharpe, Christina. 2016. *In the wake: On blackness and being*. Durham: Duke University Press.

Smith, Sidonie, and Julia Watson. 1996. *Getting a life: Everyday uses of autobiography*. Minneapolis: University of Minnesota Press.

Snooks, Gina, and Sonja Boon. 2017. Salt fish and molasses: Unsettling the palate in the spaces between two continents. *European Journal of Life Writing* 6: 218–241. https://doi.org/10.4362/ejlw.6.213.

Spry, Tami. 2001. Performing autoethnography: An embodied methodological praxis. *Qualitative Inquiry* 7 (6): 706–732.

———. 2009. Bodies of/and evidence. *International Review of Qualitative Research* 1 (4): 603–610.

———. 2011. *Body, paper, stage: Writing and performing autoethnography.* Walnut Creek: Left Coast Press.

———. 2016. *Autoethnography and the other: Unsettling power through utopian performatives.* London and New York: Routledge.

Tsalach, Calanit. 2013. Between silence and speech: Autoethnography as an otherness-resisting practice. *Qualitative Inquiry* 19 (2): 71–80. https://doi.org/10.1177/1077800412462986.

Tuck, Eve, and C. Ree. 2013. A glossary of haunting. In *Handbook of autoethnography,* ed. Stacey Holman Jones, Tony E. Adams, and Carolyn Ellis, 639–658. Walnut Creek: Left Coast Press.

Tye, Diane. 2010. *Baking as biography: A life story in recipes.* Montreal and Kingston: McGill-Queen's University Press.

Walker, Lawrence R., and Peter Bellingham. 2011. *Island environments in a changing world.* Cambridge: Cambridge University Press.

Waterston, Elizabeth. 2000. The iconography of islands: Margaret Atwood and L. M. Montogmery. In *Message in a bottle: The literature of small islands,* ed. Laurie Brinklow, Frank Ledwell, and Jane Ledwell, 265–276. Charlottetown: Institute for Island Studies.

Webb-Campbell, Shannon. 2017. The call of the Atlantic. *NQ Online.* http://nqonline.ca/article/the-atlantics-call-and-response/. Accessed 30 Aug 2017.

Woolf, Virginia. 1988. *A room of one's own.* London: Grafton Books.

Zilmer, Kristel. 2012. The powers and purposes of an insular setting: On source motifs in Old-Norse literature. In *Isolated islands in medieval nature, culture and mind,* ed. Torstein Jørgensen and Gerhard Jaritz, 22–35. Budapest and New York: Central European University Press.

PART 1

Origins

CHAPTER 2

Myths: Fishy

Abstract This essay situates mermaids—fish women—as openings to trans histories in Newfoundland. It develops narratives of human-fish relations at both material and metaphoric levels, considering settler, Indigenous, Black, and trans engagements with fish, fishiness, and fishy being. Ultimately, this essay argues for a trans fishy subjectivity attentive and responsive to the multiple ontological histories and trajectories at the nexus of sense, self, settler, sex, and species.

Keywords Mermaid • Trans • Fish • Fish pluralities • Fishy subjectivity

In January 2017, I first discovered a well-known archival engraving of mermaids in St. John's harbour. With exquisite detail, it presents an encounter between three mermaids and a group of European colonizers at a Newfoundland shoreline. Even though the colonizers appear to be terrified, the mermaids reach toward them with open arms, as if to introduce their watery ways of being to the terrestrial strangers. The work itself has slippery origins: while it is attributed to Theodor de Bry, who died in 1598, it is based on a violent account described in *A discourse and discovery of Newfoundland* (1620) by Sir Richard Whitbourne, the grandfather of Newfoundland and Labrador's settler colonial history.

© The Author(s) 2018
S. Boon et al., *Autoethnography and Feminist Theory at the Water's Edge*, https://doi.org/10.1007/978-3-319-90829-8_2

Mermaids are queer figures in Newfoundland and Labrador history; they appear only in tiny bursts and then disappear for centuries. They are misunderstood, physically assaulted, and forced to vanish (Whitbourne 1620). In this place, mermaids and trans women are connected. We mutate across species and sex (Hayward 2010); we are hybrid and hyphenated kin (Wah 2006; Haraway 2016). Captivated by our shared histories (erased, fishy, and imagined), I interrogate my own hybrid body—a trans, island body—and its place in Newfoundland's historical past. As I continue to encounter what can be read as a confluence of mermaid realities, legends, and archival touches, and building on Astrida Neimanis' argument that humans have "fishy beginnings" (2017, 109), I suggest that hybrid embodiments of Newfoundland womanhood (fish woman or trans woman) have watery pasts and potentialities. Ultimately, however, I arrive at a moment of questioning where these pasts may lead. Forming linkages between the labour of Atlantic women islanders, Black queer vernacular in diaspora, Indigenous human-animal relations, and trans phenomenology is, I argue, one way to highlight and trouble posthuman fishy futures for trans women's lives in Newfoundland and Labrador.

Settler relations with fish in Newfoundland stretch back hundreds of years. On and offshore, fish are political and economic beings (Probyn 2016), and they can be mapped most significantly through a series of historical coordinates and positions: the island's initial colonization at the close of the fifteenth century, merchant trade and commerce right up to the 1900s, everyday labour and life in coastal communities, and the collapse of the Atlantic cod fishery in 1992. Fish have shaped slippery ontologies (Law and Lien 2012; Todd 2014) for white settler islanders. Indeed, Newfoundland and Labrador Heritage states that "it was fish that brought Europeans [here], it was fish that dictated the pattern of their settlement, and it was the catching, salting, drying, and marketing of fish that laid down the forms and structures of the society they built" (2015, para 1). Although the labour of fish relations in Newfoundland has historically been associated with settler masculinities (Hallett 2016), feminist scholars have recently recorded women's multiplex ties to fish, including the catching, preservation, and preparation of cod (Cullum 2003; Ennis and Woodrow 1996; Grzetic 2002; McCay 1995; Murray 1980; Power 1997; Robbins 1997).

Indigenous relations to fish have been documented primarily in Labrador, the 'other' portion of provincial space that is home to the Inuit and Innu peoples, as well as to the Southern Inuit of NunatuKavut (Arendt

2010; Calder et al. 2016; Samson and Pretty 2006). As a white islander and settler, I cannot make claims about Indigenous worlds and worldviews; rather it is my anti-colonial responsibility to engage with, learn from, and share Indigenous theories and perspectives. My reading of human-fish scholarship in Labrador makes connections with Zoe Todd's "'fish pluralities' (multiple ways of knowing and defining fish)" (2014, 217), in Paulatuuq, Arctic Canada. For Todd, situating fish as environmental and historical actors, and understanding "fish-as-political-citizens" (2017, 109) opens up an arena for theorizing the political kinship of human and more-than-human lives in northern Canada (2014, 217). Todd suggests that everyday life for the Paulatuuqmiut (people from Paulatuuq) is fishy: it ranges from catching and preparing fish, to forming art and philosophies with fish (2014, 222). From this posture, I question how fishy realities might be understood for both settlers and Indigenous peoples, particularly trans or two-spirit women, in Newfoundland and Labrador.

As I have grown to learn what trans subjectivity and corporeality mean in my life, I have encountered vernacular terms and various forms of cultural production that shape the way I move through the world. 'Fishy' is a term I first learned from engaging with Black drag/queer/trans media, and it has morphed into a linguistic trace I use frequently with other (settler) trans women in Newfoundland. To 'be fishy' or to 'serve fish' involves passing as cis women, or performing an ambiguous or suspicious 'ultra-femininity.' While the use of 'fish' as an ontological performative has been critiqued in and outside of Black queer and trans communities, Philip Hayward notes that there are unresolved debates about the many queer, slippery, and problematic uses of 'fish' (2017b, 49). Even though there is a small body of scholarly material exploring explicit relations between 'fish' and trans/gender variant embodiments (Hayward 2008, 2011; Hayward 2017b; Rosario 2014; Simmons 2014), I have not discovered any scholarship concerned with 'fish' as a vernacular measure of trans women's subjectivities, or as a posthuman representation of trans lives.

How might 'fish' be trans through their wave-like flux and movements across racial and spatial borders? Writing a racial poetics of transatlantic water, Dora Silva Santana (2017) weaves together enslaved ancestries, trans embodiments, and wet ways of knowing. When she writes of "ancestors who transitioned through the water, into the water, from the water" (2017, 187), she illustrates the diasporic and interstitial ontologies of the Middle Passage, wherein millions of African peoples were entrapped and transported across the Atlantic Ocean—like fish—to be traded. Becoming animal and becoming enslaved, in this way, contemporary uses of 'fish' are haunted (Brand 2001; Tuck and Ree 2013) processes of "l/anguish"-ing (Philip 2015, 56). They reflect upon both a foreign, diasporic language (Sheth 2014), and the continuous racist lacerations endured and resisted by queer and trans people of color.

Black theorists illustrate that the category 'human' has, since the Enlightenment, not been accessible to those with African ancestries. Consequently, a growing body of Black theory engages with questions of the hum-animal, articulating racial post- and inhumanisms for Black futures (Bey 2017; Hayward 2017a; Warren 2017; Wynter 2003). On these grounds, can Black futures be fishy? For white trans women, to 'pass' with an appropriated fishy ontology—to be seen as cisgender—is to be recognized as 'real.' However, as Santana argues, 'passing' promises no safety for Black trans women (2017, 185). If we, white settler trans women, are to understand ourselves as being fishy, we must recognize our own performances of what Hélène Cixous and Catherine Clément call "surreptitious slippage" (1986, 79) across species, race, sex, and history— keeping our own slimy secrets of trans being, while many Black trans women face violence and death (Hayward 2017a; Krell 2017), and Indigenous communities, ecosystems, and worldviews are threatened, poisoned, and destroyed (Calder et al. 2016; Cruikshank 2005).

Certainly, scholars and writers have examined affective, hybrid, linguistic, and transgenic cross-species encounters between humans and fishy beings (Bahng 2015; Hayward 2011; Kelley and Hayward 2013; Lai 2002; Todd 2014, 2017). Fishiness is manifest with linguistic dilemmas: the use and appropriation of Black queer vernacular, discursive divisions between Indigenous and settler conceptualizations of nature, and the misclassification of various aquatic creatures (jellyfish and starfish) as fish. For instance, Eva Hayward writes connections between the sensuous, immersive matters of jellyfish, starfish, and trans embodiments, illustrating a permeable form of (non)fishy being (2011, 265; see also Hayward 2008). When she writes of sensual connections between humans and jellies, and the shared technoscientific transness of jellies and trans women (2011, 267, 271), she draws parallels with Todd's fish pluralities—showing that trans as a coordination, as a way of mattering, or as a sensuous and reflexive figuration, is performed, in part, through multiple movements across species and sex in varying nature-cultures.

Attentive to these movements, a *fishy subjectivity* for trans women in Newfoundland and Labrador must be an expression to "turn, bend, or reflect back upon" (Turner 1988, 24) colonial and settler relations with fish in provincial history. It must also engage with Indigenous and Black conceptions/dialectics of fish. In my life, writing, theorizing, and living with a fishy subjectivity forms a cartography of belonging (see also Chaps. 11 and 17), whereby creatively mapping 'fish' across history, race, species, and sex changes the way I navigate life as a trans woman islander. A fishy subjectivity recognizes an assemblage of (non)fishy slippery ontologies: queer fish, trans fish, serving fish, fish-as-beings, salt fish, feesh, transgenic fish, entrapped fish, performative fish, phallic fish, fish woman, starfish, jellyfish, disappearing/dying fish (see also Chap. 3). Alongside Neimanis' stretching back to oceanic pasts, and Santana's wet sensibility between oceans and optics—"eyes see, eyes sea, see, sea, see-sea-eye" (2017, 188)—I envision a fishy formulation between sense, settler, self, sex, and species, through which trans women in Newfoundland can imagine futures that continue to swim against the current.

[DJ]

References

Arendt, Beatrix. 2010. Caribou to cod: Moravian missionary influence on Inuit subsistence strategies. *Historical Archaeology* 44 (3): 81–101. https://doi.org/10.1007/BF03376805.

Bahng, Aimee. 2015. Specters of the Pacific: Salt fish drag and atomic hauntologies in the era of genetic modification. *Journal of American Studies* 49 (4): 663–683. https://doi.org/10.1017/S0021875815001668.

Bey, Marquis. 2017. The trans*-ness of blackness, the blackness of trans*-ness. *TSQ: Transgender Studies Quarterly* 4 (2): 275–295. https://doi.org/10.1215/23289252-3815069.

Brand, Dionne. 2001. *A map to the Door of No Return: Notes to belonging*. Toronto: Vintage Canada.

Calder, Ryan S.D., et al. 2016. Future impacts of hydroelectric power development on methylmercury exposures of Canadian Indigenous communities. *Environmental Science & Technology* 50 (23): 13115–13122. https://doi.org/10.1021/acs.est.6b04447.

Cixous, Hélène, and Catherine Clément. 1986. Sorties: Out and out: Attacks/ ways out/forays. In *The newly born woman*, Trans. Betsy Wing, 63–132. Minneapolis: University of Minnesota Press.

Cruikshank, Julie. 2005. *Do glaciers speak?: Local knowledge, colonial encounters, and social imagination*. Vancouver: UBC Press.

Cullum, Linda. 2003. *Narratives at work: Women, men, unionization, and the fashioning of identities*. St. John's: ISER Books.

Ennis, Frances, and Helen Woodrow. 1996. *Strong as the ocean: Women's work in the Newfoundland and Labrador fisheries*. St. John's: Harrish Press.

Grzetic, Brenda. 2002. Between life and death: Women fish harvesters in Newfoundland and Labrador. MA Thesis, Memorial University of Newfoundland.

Hallett, Vicki. 2016. Cold water cowboys and Newfoundland masculinity. *Acadiensis*. https://acadiensis.wordpress.com/2016/06/13/cold-water-cowboys-and-newfoundland-masculinity. Accessed 18 Mar 2018.

Haraway, Donna. 2016. *Staying with the trouble: Making kin in the Chthulucene*. Durham: Duke University Press.

Hayward, Eva. 2008. More lessons from a starfish: Prefixial flesh and transspeciated selves. *Women's Studies Quarterly* 36 (3–4): 64–85. https://doi.org/10.1353/wsq.0.0099.

———. 2010. Spider city sex. *Women & Performance: A Journal of Feminist Theory* 20 (3): 225–251. https://doi.org/10.1080/0740770X.2010.529244.

———. 2011. Ciliated sense. In *Theorizing animals: Re-thinking humanimal relations*, ed. Nik Taylor and Tania Signal, 255–280. Leiden: Brill.

———. 2017a. Don't exist. *TSQ: Transgender Studies Quarterly* 4 (2): 191–194. https://doi.org/10.1215/23289252-3814985.

Hayward, Philip. 2017b. *Making a splash: Mermaids (and mer-men) in 20th and 21st century audiovisual media*. Bloomington: Indiana University Press.

Kelley, Lindsay, and Eva Hayward. 2013. Carnal light. *Parallax* 19 (1): 114–127. https://doi.org/10.1080/13534645.2013.743297.

Krell, Elías Cosenza. 2017. Is transmisogyny killing trans women of color? Black trans feminisms and the exigencies of white femininity. *TSQ: Transgender Studies Quarterly* 4 (2): 226–242. https://doi.org/10.1215/23289252-3815033.

Lai, Larissa. 2002. *Salt fish girl*. Toronto: Thomas Allen Publishers.

Law, John, and Marianne Elisabeth Lien. 2012. Slippery: Field notes in empirical ontology. *Social Studies of Science* 43 (3): 363–378. https://doi.org/10.1177/0306312712456947.

McCay, Bonnie J. 1995. Fish guts, hair nets and unemployment stamps: Women and work in co-operative fish plants. In *Their lives and times: Women in Newfoundland and Labrador, a collage*, ed. Carmelita McGrath, Barbara Neis, and Marilyn Porter, 144–162. St John's, NL: Killick Press.

Murray, Hilda Chaulk. 1980. *More than 50%: A woman's life in a Newfoundland outport, 1900–1950*. St. John's, NL: Flanker Press.

Neimanis, Astrida. 2017. *Bodies of water: Posthuman feminist phenomenology*. Sydney: Bloomsbury.

Newfoundland and Labrador Heritage. 2015. Fisheries. http://www.heritage.nf.ca/articles/economy/fishery.php. Accessed 14 July 2017.

Philip, M. NourbeSe. 2015. Discourse on the logic of language. In *She tries her tongue, her silence softly breaks*, 55–60. Charlottetown: Ragweed Press.

Power, Nicole Gerarda. 1997. Women, processing industries and the environment: A sociological analysis of women fish and crab processing workers' local ecological knowledge. MA Thesis, Memorial University of Newfoundland.

Probyn, Elspeth. 2016. *Eating the ocean*. Durham: Duke University Press.

Robbins, Nancy. 1997. Images and realities: Women's experiences in a Newfoundland and Labrador fishery crisis. MA Thesis, Memorial University of Newfoundland.

Rosario, Vernon A. 2014. Studs, stems, and fishy boys: Adolescent Latino gender variance and the slippery diagnosis of transsexuality. In *Transgender experience: Place, ethnicity, and visibility*, ed. Chantal Zabus and David Coad, 51–67. New York: Routledge.

Samson, Colin, and Jules Pretty. 2006. Environmental and health benefits of hunting lifestyles and diets for the Innu of Labrador. *Food Policy* 31 (6): 528–553. https://doi.org/10.1016/j.foodpol.2006.02.001.

Santana, Dora Silva. 2017. Transitionings and returnings: Experiments with the poetics of transatlantic water. *TSQ: Transgender Studies Quarterly* 4 (2): 181–190. https://doi.org/10.1215/23289252-3814973.

Sheth, Falguni A. 2014. Interstitiality: Making space for migration, diaspora, and racial complexity. *Hypatia* 29 (1): 75–93. https://doi.org/10.1111/hypa.12075.

Simmons, Nathaniel. 2014. Speaking like a queen in *Rupaul's Drag Race*: Towards a speech code of American drag queens. *Sexuality & Culture* 18: 630–648. https://doi.org/10.1007/s12119-013-9213-2.

Todd, Zoe. 2014. Fish pluralities: Human-animals relations and sites of engagement in Paulatuuq, Arctic Canada. *Études/Inuit/Studies* 38 (1–2): 217–238. https://doi.org/10.7202/1028861ar.

———. 2017. Fish, kin and hope: Tending to water violations in *Amiskwaciwâskahikan* and Treaty Six territory. *Afterall: A Journal of Art, Context and Enquiry* 43 (1): 103–107. https://doi.org/10.1086/692559.

Tuck, Eve, and C. Ree. 2013. A glossary of haunting. In *Handbook of autoethnography*, ed. Stacey Holman Jones, Tony E. Adams, and Carolyn Ellis, 639–658. Walnut Grove: Left Coast Press.

Turner, Victor. 1988. *The anthropology of performance*. New York: Performing Arts Journal Publications.

Wah, Fred. 2006. *Diamond grill*. Edmonton: NeWest Press.

Warren, Calvin. 2017. Calling into being tranifestation, black trans, and the problem of ontology. *TSQ: Transgender Studies Quarterly* 4 (2): 266–274. https://doi.org/10.1215/23289252-3815057.

Whitbourne, Richard. 1620. *A discourse and discovery of Newfoundland*. London: Felix Kingston.

Wynter, Sylvia. 2003. Unsettling the coloniality of being/power/truth/freedom: Toward the human, after man, its overrepresentation—An argument. *CR: The New Centennial Review* 3 (3): 257–337. https://doi.org/10.1353/ncr.2004.0015.

CHAPTER 3

Hauntings: Love

Abstract What does it mean to love fish? This chapter, a meditation on love, considers the space of encounter between the human and the more-than-human. Drawing on the work of Elspeth Probyn, Karin Amimoto Ingersoll, Sara Ahmed, Luce Irigaray, Eve Tuck and C. Ree, it examines the profoundly embodied intimacy of human-fish relations, developing the idea of love through the lens of grief, mourning, loss, and haunting.

Keywords Fish • Love • Mourning • Loss • Grief

Fish was never part of my childhood imagination; as a prairie-raised child, my inner landscape was shaped by wheat, beef, mosquitoes, and the endlessness of a brilliant blue sky. The sea entered my world only in second-hand sorts of ways: the oily landscape of a tin of smoked oysters, the briny, salty, tangy, and sweet slither of pickled herring. Many years later, after moving to Vancouver, I learned that fish farmers could cultivate the pink of their salmon. I love fish, I said, but what was that love? And how could I begin to know it?

It took island living to understand fishy being. During a summer in Barbados visiting relatives, I communed with sand dollars and sea urchins, shaped my body alongside seaweed, and flitted through the water with tiny fishy beings. I got tangled in a riptide, my body tossing and tumbling in a rush of sound. Later, a jellyfish stretched itself along my arm, its

© The Author(s) 2018   25
S. Boon et al., *Autoethnography and Feminist Theory at the Water's Edge*, https://doi.org/10.1007/978-3-319-90829-8_3

deflated blue body, like a chewed up wad of gum, extending tentacles that reached from my fingertips to my shoulders. That summer when I was eleven, I became ocean, I became fish. Slippery. Watery. Salted.

How might a fishy thinking animate feminist thought? What does it mean to love fish? And how might such love move us towards different ways of being in the world? Living in Newfoundland has brought all of this to the fore. It's 2018. Just over twenty-five years ago, in 1992, the federal government imposed the cod moratorium. There were no more fish. Where once they could be gathered by the armful, the cod was gone. The oceans were empty, haunted. And so, too, were Newfoundlanders, their fishy selves searching, yearning, longing for fish (Delisle 2013; Chafe 2008; Neis 2005; Murray 1980; Overton 1996). "In Cod We Trust(ed)," reads a poster in one of the tourist shops in downtown St. John's. The fishing stages are silent. Island identity, it seems, has never fully recovered.

On this island, fishy thinking is visceral thinking. "I just loves the fish," states a woman participant in a 1986 study of the Newfoundland fishery (Davis 1986, 134). Fishy thinking is about fingers that still bleed fish, about bodies scarred with the labour of making fish, about century-old storehouses that still leech salt. How to understand a fishy embodiment in the absence of fish? What does it mean to love fish when the fish are gone? Karin Amimoto Ingersoll offers the possibility of a seascape epistemology, an approach to knowing that is premised on "the ocean and the wind as an interconnected system that allows for successful navigation through them" (2016, 6). A seascape epistemology is about interactions and relationships, about knowing home within the context of movement (2016, 6). Here in Newfoundland, that seascape epistemology is a fishy epistemology, an epistemology of grief, mourning, and silence.

If the ocean is haunted by the silent memory of fish (Probyn 2016, 27), then the fishing body, too, is a haunted body. To love fish is to carry the knowledge of fish deep inside the body, to long for the absent touch of fish. It is to be a watery body gasping on land. A fishy thinking is to know the ocean intimately, to carry it on the skin (Neimanis 2017; Probyn 2001; Prosser 2001; see also Chap. 2) and in the very flesh of the self. But more than this, fishy thinking is about mobility; it locates us not in the groundedness of the "terroir," but rather, in the ever-moving currents of the "merroir" (Probyn 2016, 52), of an ocean that rises and falls.

Fishy thinking asks me to move differently, to imagine my legs as fins, my neck growing gills. I glide, slide, my body always buffeted by waves. Fishy thinking changes my understanding of borders and boundaries.

Who am I, as fish? My scales glitter in the sun, but outside the water, I find that I gasp; I cannot breathe. As fish, I swim; I am ocean, my salted body buoyant in the waves.

I am interested here in mourning and grief in relation to love. Where the body itself grieves. I want to think of fish not just as commodity, but as identity, encounter, being-with (Probyn 2016). In a fishy thinking, we world with fish (Neimanis and Walker 2014). Love, here, emerges at the point of encounter, the place of splitting (Kristeva 2000), the *entredeux* (Cixous and Calle-Gruber 1997) where meaning collapses. Becoming fish becoming human becoming fish. But what happens when the fish are no longer? What is a fishy subjectivity with a haunted fish, a ghostly ocean, a memory of encounter? What does it mean to *love* fish?

Love might be understood in multiple ways. Sara Ahmed, referencing Levinas, proposes the idea of proximity, an encounter that does not integrate or incorporate the other into the self, but through which our selves are mutually constituted in a space of shared breathing (2000, 140). Love, in this way, acts as a mediator, a space between. In the words of Luce Irigaray, "In an exchange between two, meaning quivers and always remains unstable, incomplete, unsettled, irreducible to the word" (2002, 28). Love, then, is always mobile, always sparking connections. Constantly reconfiguring itself, love is a continual becoming, a mutual worlding (Neimanis and Walker 2014).

Foundational to love is the idea of touch, of skin. Skin is "testimony" (Probyn 2001, 87); "the body's memory of our lives" (Prosser 2001, 52), it holds all of our encounters. The ghostly whisper of the jellyfish, the sandpaper scars of the riptide, the shimmering scales of cod. As the site of longing, yearning, and desire, skin is where human and fish come together: blood, scales, memories, tears. "We are," writes Quinn Eades, "narrative mapped onto flesh" (2015, 229). Skin is where love is made, in the memory of the touch, the whisper of our shared breathing.

In a Newfoundland context, love is necessarily about haunting; it is the memory of fish, the ghost of a touch. "Haunting," the silent oceans remind us, "is the cost of subjugation" (Tuck and Ree 2013, 643). Making fish, making love is about making theory at the water's edge, listening to the ocean, watching the sky, feeling the wind. *What does it mean to love fish?* Making fish, making love is the touch of the ocean in the shape of cod, skin and desire coming together as one.

[SB]

REFERENCES

Ahmed, Sara. 2000. *Strange encounters: Embodied others in post-coloniality.* London: Routledge.

Amimoto Ingersoll, Karin. 2016. *Waves of knowing: A seascape epistemology.* Durham: Duke University Press.

Chafe, Paul. 2008. Only an artist could measure up to such a place: Place and identity in Newfoundland literature. Ph.D. dissertation. Memorial University, St. John's.

Cixous, Hélène, and Mireille Calle-Gruber. 1997. *Hélène Cixous, Rootprints: Memory and life writing.* Trans. Eric Prenowitz. London and New York: Routledge.

Davis, Dona Lee. 1986. Occupational community and fishermen's wives in a Newfoundland fishing village. *Anthropological Quarterly* 59 (3): 129–142.

Delisle, Jennifer Bowering. 2013. *The Newfoundland diaspora: Mapping the literature of out-migration.* Waterloo: Wilfrid Laurier University Press.

Eades, Quinn. 2015. *All the beginnings: A queer autobiography of the body.* Melbourne: Tantanoola.

Irigaray, Luce. 2002. *The way of love.* Trans. Heidi Bostic and Stephen Pluhácek. London: Continuum.

Kristeva, Julia. 2000. Motherhood [according to Giovanni Bellini]. In *French feminism reader,* ed. Kelly Oliver, 176–180. Lanham: Rowman & Littlefield.

Murray, Hilda Chaulk. 1980. *More than 50%: A woman's life in a Newfoundland outport, 1900–1950.* St. John's, NL: Flanker Press.

Neimanis, Astrida. 2017. *Bodies of water: Posthuman feminist phenomenology.* London: Bloomsbury Academic.

Neimanis, Astrida, and Rachel Loewen Walker. 2014. Weathering: Climate change and the 'thick time' of transcorporeality. *Hypatia* 29 (3): 558–575. https://doi.org/10.1111/hypa.12064.

Neis, Barbara. 2005. *Changing tides: Gender, fisheries and globalization.* Halifax: Fernwood.

Overton, James. 1996. *Making a world of difference: Essays on tourism, culture and development in Newfoundland.* St. John's: ISER.

Probyn, Elspeth. 2001. Eating skin. In *Thinking through the skin,* ed. Sara Ahmed and Jackie Stacey, 87–103. London and New York: Routledge.

———. 2016. *Eating the ocean.* Durham: Duke University Press.

Prosser, Jay. 2001. Skin memories. In *Thinking through the skin,* ed. Sara Ahmed and Jackie Stacey, 52–68. London and New York: Routledge.

Tuck, Eve, and C. Ree. 2013. A glossary of haunting. In *Handbook of autoethnography,* ed. Stacey Holman Jones, Tony E. Adams, and Carolyn Ellis, 639–658. Walnut Grove: Left Coast Press.

CHAPTER 4

Histories: Roots

Abstract This chapter tangles with origins, histories, and genealogies, considering roots not only as a powerful metaphor, but also, in the case of prematurely grey hair, as genetic inheritance. Drawing on the work of Toni Morrison, Gilles Deleuze and Félix Guattari, and Quinn Eades, among others, the essay engages with roots at both material and mythical levels, looking in particular at how roots might be unsettled and uprooted, the site of new beginnings as well as ancestral longings.

Keywords Roots • Rhizome • Origins • Body • Genetic inheritance

I found my first grey hair when I was sixteen. I recall peering at the mirror of my father's pickup truck as he drove me to school, only to be struck with disbelief at my reflection. I didn't want to be dramatic about something as seemingly insignificant as a rogue hair follicle, but I couldn't help but feel somehow out of place. Out of time. Who goes grey at sixteen? I hoped it was a mere anomaly, and carried on with my day, but over the course of the next few months, more and more strands of grey started sprouting along the top of my forehead. I'd never been interested in dying my hair before, but my embarrassment eventually led me to the hair salon. The dye settled into my roots and restored me to a full brunette, and I finally felt like I had control over my body. But as anyone who has dyed their hair knows, this was only a temporary solution. As the weeks passed,

© The Author(s) 2018
S. Boon et al., *Autoethnography and Feminist Theory at the Water's Edge*, https://doi.org/10.1007/978-3-319-90829-8_4

the grey started growing back, unsettling my hairline once again. The dye—and indeed, my time and my budget—were no match for those inevitable roots.

While roots in the literal sense have their place in more scientific pursuits, their popularity within not only academic, but also everyday language suggests the pervasive power of roots as metaphor (Buttimer 1984; Tuan 1984; Wampole 2016). The imagery of plant roots, web-like and ever-reaching through the depths of a soil-based home, has long garnered comparisons to questions of identity, belonging, and ancestral history. More specifically, the popular notion of family trees marries a sense of interconnectedness with a historically-founded sense of rootedness through roots and branches. Toni Morrison (2008) has written on the foundation of rootedness for Black Americans in particular, whereby roots connect one directly, and necessarily, to the ancestors. Gilles Deleuze and Félix Guattari (1987) have also famously expanded on the root metaphor, offering the imagery of rhizomes to emphasize the complexity and nonlinear nature of roots and rootedness. Much of this thinking on roots remains conceptual in nature, metaphoric from start to finish. But what happens when we bring the body into the conversation? How do we make sense of the material *and* the mythical within our storied roots?

Considering roots through seemingly foreign roots or rhizomes creates the illusion that our past is separate from our present, and from our own selves. However, the roots of our past permeate both the present and the future (Stoler 2008, 194; see also Grosz 2000). After all, as Elizabeth Grosz observes, "the future is the domain of what endures" (2000, 1018); what endures of the past exists through its "capacity to become something other" (Grosz 2000, 1018). The past, then, is always a becoming. As roots grow, they also change. Through time and place, Deleuze and Guattari suggest, "the root's unity subsists, as past or yet to come, as possible" (1987, 5). How does history seep into the stories we tell today? How does the past permeate our bodies? Roots, both material and metaphoric, help represent the complex nexus of history, origin, self, family, and the stories that hold it all together.

It took me a long time to get used to seeing silver streaks in my reflection. Despite my desire to attribute a more philosophical or prophetic meaning to my hair, the reality was much more prosaic: my roots were a genetic inheritance. I soon learned that my grandfather Cooper, too, had developed a streak of grey as a teenager. Because I was quite young when he died, I hadn't remembered this detail about him. But a journey through old photo albums—what Juan Carlos Pita Castro might call our "archipela-goes" of "aggregated memories" (2014, 153)—confirmed that we indeed shared this silver mark (see also Cixous and Calle-Gruber 1997, 179). Through photographic ruins and rootprints, this genealogical journey confronted me with "the implausible origin with a spike" (Cixous and Calle-Gruber 1997, 187). The past, no longer confined to the worn borders of a photo, bleeds into my body, piercing the present with histories waiting to be known, stories waiting to be told. Those grey roots did not feel so foreign anymore. Instead, they felt like history.

Often, we think of these roots in terms of ancestral connections, a family tree with roots reaching across foreign or familiar lands. Across time. But what happens to this family tree when we turn to our own bodies? Simone de Beauvoir has suggested that our bodies are "the instrument of our grasp upon the world" (qtd. in Boon 2017, 191). Similarly, Sonja Boon suggests, "the past can tell us stories about our bodies and further, our bodies, even living in the present day, can tell us stories about our pasts" (2017, 187). What stories can my roots tell?

Hélène Cixous would argue that our roots "have always been there," whether we look to them or not (Cixous and Calle-Gruber 1997, 179). Sure enough, whether or not I disguised them with dye, the genealogical reality of my roots would always be there. And so, writing through this body, about this body, "I grab on to the roots, the DNA of my family tree" and take a journey through their (hi)stories (Spry 2016, 72). As perplexing as they may be, my roots are forever growing, their presence a reminder that the past is perpetually present—through the material, through myth, through memory (Cixous and Calle-Gruber 1997, 179).

Quinn Eades imagines the act of writing creating a "vast root system […] that spawns all bodies" (2015, 25). Inspired by Deleuze and Guattari's (1987) expansive web of rhizomes, Eades' root system is complex, fragmented, mosaic by nature (2015, 27). For Eades, writing the body—and the body, writing—is forever a becoming, "the telling of a story, not the story told" (2015, 15). But to what extent is the writing of a body the writing of a self? When I write about my body, am I telling the story of my grandfather, or the story of me? Perhaps I am telling both. Or perhaps, neither. After all, stories are always an interaction between seer and seen (Butler 2005; Spry 2016). As Judith Butler suggests, "The stories do not capture the body to which they refer. Even the history of this body is not fully narratable" (Butler 2005, 38). Between self and other is the "*unsettled-I*" (Spry 2016, 77; italics original), where the "I" is both constructed and complicated by our relations with others (Minh-ha 1989, 22, 90).

Our stories exist not entirely for ourselves, but in and through the count-less stories of every Other we encounter (Butler 2005, 8; see also Spry 2016; Minh-ha 1989).

When people ask about the origins of my silver streak—"Do you dye it that way? *Where* does it come from?"—my usual response is: "It's genetic. It came from my grandfather." But is that enough? Where did it originally "come from"? How deep do the roots grow? The stories I tell may differ from those that others conjure for me. And still, stretching beneath the surface, are others that remain untold. When we dig up our roots, what remains undug (Eades 2015, 27)? As I re/map my body—as I dig through my roots—the stories I tell will change through time, a continual becom-ing through place, through language.

How far must we dig before there is nothing left? Where is the origin of the root? If we find ourselves at the reaches of our root tips, and at the depths of our rootprints (Cixous and Calle-Gruber 1997), would we find ourselves at a beginning, or at an ending? After all, as Dionne Brand observes, "all origins are arbitrary" (Brand 2001, 64; see also Chap. 11). Michel Foucault similarly considers origins not as fixed, but as fragmented (Foucault 1977, 142). History is thus needed "to dispel the chimeras of origins" (Foucault 1977, 144). Following this, we might say that the pur-pose of digging our roots is not to reach a destination. Rather, the process itself becomes our origin story. If, as Eades suggests, the "story is the body's genesis," then the body's beginning must be both behind and ahead (Eades 2015, 128). As Butler argues, even as we narrate our origin stories, those stories necessarily change with each telling (Butler 2005, 37). This is not a defect of narration, but rather, a necessary characteristic that represents the complexity of self, of other, and of becomings—through the body, through history, and through stories themselves. We change, stories change, and stories change us. And still, there are the stories, the origins, that remain untouched, undug, nestled deep within the rhizomatic web of history.

If roots represent our family histories—and our bodily stories—then we must also consider how roots help us navigate our sense of place. In this untangling of our histories, where is it that we dig? Where are our roots (Castro 2014, 168)? Here, on my island home, a sense of rootedness tends to rely on white settler histories (see Chap. 17). But how much of our genealogical and geographical search for origins considers the colonial implications upon place, race, or history (Nash 2003, 181; see also Minh-ha 1989, 89)? Despite pride in 'our' island/ness, digging up our roots becomes more important than ever. But if we wish to learn—about ourselves and about others—we cannot merely revere the root. Sometimes it is necessary to expose them, to prune them, and to examine the "guts of historicities pulled out by the roots" (Spry 2016, 72). The past is not passive; rather, it is unsettled. History persists through the stories we tell. But as people change, so do our stories. They grow and stretch, reaching through time and place. Like roots, they navigate, adapt, and absorb, forever changing along with their surroundings. What (hi)stories will our rootings and uprootings tell? And which ones are silenced? What stories remain untold, or perhaps, unheard?

The further we dig in our search for origins, the more stories we unearth, and the more stories we create. To trace my roots—to trace the genealogical germination of grey—is to explore the stories of relation, of connection and chaos (Butler 2005, 8; Spry 2016, 76–7). To dig is to write (Eades 2015, 128). And as we keep digging, we find love, memory, trauma, desire, dreams (Eades 2015, 26; see also Chap. 18). We find a ceaseless (rhizo)sphere of stories to tell. Roots continue to grow, but we can try to untangle them, to uproot them once in a while. Shake off the soil and share our stories. For just when we think we have an ending, we are only ever just beginning.

[LB]

References

Boon, Sonja. 2017. Minuet as method: Embodied performance in the research process. In *Methodological challenges in nature-culture and environmental history research*, ed. Jocelyn Thorpe, Stephanie Rutherford, and L. Anders Sandberg, 187–199. New York: Routledge.

Brand, Dionne. 2001. *A map to the Door of No Return: Notes to belonging.* Toronto: Vintage Canada.

Butler, Judith. 2005. *Giving an account of oneself.* New York: Fordham University Press.

Buttimer, Anne. 1984. Musing on Helicon: Root metaphors and geography. In *Place: Experience and symbol*, ed. Miles Richardson, 55–62. Baton Rouge: Geoscience Publications, Dept. of Geography and Anthropology, Louisiana State University.

Castro, Juan Carlos Pita. 2014. Interrelations between narration, identity and place. In *Embodied narratives: Connecting stories, bodies, cultures and ecologies*, ed. Laura Formenti, Linden West, and Marianne Horsdal, 149–171. Odense: University Press of Southern Denmark; European Society for Research on the Education of Adults (ESREA) Life History and Biography Network.

Cixous, Hélène, and Mireille Calle-Gruber. 1997. *Hélène Cixous, Rootprints: Memory and life writing*. Trans. Eric Prenowitz. New York: Routledge.

Deleuze, Gilles, and Félix Guattari. 1987. *A thousand plateaus: Capitalism and schizophrenia*. Minneapolis: University of Minnesota Press.

Eades, Quinn. 2015. *All the beginnings: A queer autobiography of the body*. Tantanoola: North Melbourne.

Foucault, Michel. 1977. *Language, counter-memory, practice: Selected essays and interviews*. Ed. Donald F. Bouchard and Trans. Donald F. Bouchard and Sherry Simon. Ithaca: Cornell University Press.

Grosz, Elizabeth. 2000. Histories of a feminist future. *Signs: Journal of Women in Culture and Society* 25 (4): 1017–1021.

Minh-ha, Trinh T. 1989. *Woman, native, other: Writing postcoloniality and feminism*. Bloomington and Indianapolis: Indiana University Press.

Morrison, Toni. 2008. *What moves at the margin: Selected nonfiction*. Ed. Carolyn C. Denard. Jackson: University Press of Mississippi.

Nash, Catherine. 2003. "'They're family!'": Cultural geographies of relatedness in popular genealogy. In *Uprootings/regroundings: Questions of home and migration*, ed. Sara Ahmed, Claudia Castañeda, Anne-Marie Fortier, and Mimi Sheller, 179–203. Oxford and New York: Berg.

Spry, Tami. 2016. *Autoethnography and the other: Unsettling power through utopian performatives*. New York and London: Routledge.

Stoler, Ann Laura. 2008. Imperial debris: Reflections on ruins and ruination. *Cultural Anthropology* 23 (2): 191–219. https://doi.org/10.1525/can.2008.23.2.191.

Tuan, Yi-Fu. 1984. In place, out of place. In *Place: Experience and symbol*, ed. Miles Richardson, 3–10. Baton Rouge: Geoscience Publications, Dept. of Geography and Anthropology, Louisiana State University.

Wampole, Christy. 2016. *Rootedness: The ramifications of a metaphor*. Chicago: University of Chicago Press.

CHAPTER 5

Memories: Mud

Abstract This chapter considers the conceptual potential of mud. A substance located at the midway point between the solid and the liquid, mud is a useful metaphor that has been central to how we have imagined human social relations. But mud is also an agentic substance, capable of articulating its own meanings. In its continual shifting, it can enable a transcorporeal politics of belonging, a model for living together in an ever-eroding, ever-shifting, constantly resurfacing world.

Keywords Mud • Transcorporeality • Stickiness • Resurfacing • Vibrant matter

July 2009. It was the summer after our first full year in Newfoundland, the summer when we started to ground ourselves in this place, to spread, reach, extend and grow our roots out across the island we had chosen to call home. Road trip, we thought. Would 3000 kilometres—from St. John's at the farthest east to L'Anse aux Meadows at the northernmost tip, and back—be enough? We packed up our car, filling every nook and cranny. Tent. Sleeping bags. Air mattresses. Cooler box. Clothes. Towels. Games. Books. And, of course, beach toys. Then we drove west, following the meandering ribbon of the Trans-Canada Highway past Clarenville, then Gander, and on through Grand Falls-Windsor towards Stephenville,

© The Author(s) 2018
S. Boon et al., *Autoethnography and Feminist Theory at the Water's Edge*, https://doi.org/10.1007/978-3-319-90829-8_5

where we turned north towards Shallow Bay Campground in Gros Morne National Park. The next day, after a lazy breakfast and a leisurely wander along a trail, we headed to the beach.

I want to think, here, about the entangled relationship between water and land, about that boundary that marks the end of islands. More specifically I want to consider mud, that substance that emerges when the two meet. At a conceptual level, mud is a useful metaphor that has been central to how we have imagined the messiness of human social relations. But mud, as vibrant matter (Bennett 2010), is also an agentic substance, capable of articulating its own meanings. What happens in this murky, interstitial space between the solid and the liquid? What might an attentiveness to mud—as both material substance and conceptual metaphor—enable? What might it mean to *play* with mud?

We deposited ourselves on the beach early in the afternoon, while the tide was out, and pulled out all of our sandcastle building supplies: shovels, rakes, pails, and sieves. What mattered most that afternoon was finding the right consistency for building. Too dry and the castle's walls would flutter into dust, too wet and they would disintegrate into themselves. The sun bore down, warming the sands of Shallow Bay. My sons and I sat there for hours, digging and constructing. Buckets for turrets, shovels to excavate moats. After the walls were up, we dug a passage right down to the ocean. In between, the kids ran along the damp sand, squealing as their toes touched the cold North Atlantic. And then, as the tide started rolling in, a castle turret leaned and collapsed. We waited and watched as the whole structure slowly dissolved, solid form melting into a thick, smooth mud.

According to the *Oxford English Dictionary*, mud is a "soft moist glutinous material made of a combination of things" ("mud, n.1"). Geologically, its consistency is never completely solid nor completely liquid; rather mud is something that brings the fluid and the solid together into a new form that blends both. More figurative definitions understand mud as something confusing, frustrating, and perplexing ("mud, n.1"). These definitions move me into the realm of Mary Douglas (1969) and Julia Kristeva (1982): mud defies order. Confounds. There is confusion, disorder, and mess here. Mud is a threat, a site of danger.

And yet, it is within the dregs, within these worthless bits, within this confusion, disorder, and mess that one must dig in order to find stories. Slinging mud, as we all know, brings mud out of the natural world and into the realm of social relations; it is about scandal and social exclusion

(McKenzie 2005). Mud is that which sticks to you and that you can't get off. A simultaneously slimy and tacky substance, mud might be understood through the work of Sara Ahmed as clingy or sticky (Ahmed 2004, 90); mud is that which you need to wash away, but which always leaves hints of itself behind. There's a troubling opacity to mud, and also an uncomfortable fleshiness. Mud stories are stories you don't want to tell, but which will be told for you. Mud stories are things that you don't want to touch, but that refuse to let you go.

At a fundamental level, mud is about encounter (Ahmed 2004, 90). As a sticky substance, mud may not necessarily be interesting in and of itself; rather, it is interesting to the extent that it interacts with other things, both human and nonhuman (Ahmed 2004; see also Tuana 2008). Mud is a point of contact. A material evocation of Kristevan abjection, it is the meeting ground between purity and danger. "What sticks," Ahmed writes, "'shows us' where the object has travelled through what it has gathered onto its surface, gatherings that become part of the object and call into question its integrity as an object" (2004, 91). Mud is thus always and already haunted. But "ghosts," Avery Gordon reminds us, "are never innocent" (1997, 22). Like mud, they make trouble. They don't follow rules. Ghosts linger, marking the past in present tense. They stick, sucking us inexorably into glutinous, complicated, uncomfortable webs of rememberings (Tuck and Ree 2013, 643). We are made and unmade by the stickiness of our encounters, the life and deathwork of our pasts inevitably haunting our presents. Playing with mud, so, too, do we become mud, our very beings also shaped by the ghosts and hauntings embedded within the muck we are navigating. I am the very mudscape upon which I cast my gaze. What stories reside in the mud at the water's edge? What stories can mud tell? What worlds are unmade through mud, and by contrast, what worlds might be made?

The viscous, writes Elizabeth Grosz, "lacks ... self-containment"; it is "a formlessness that engulfs all form, a disorder that threatens all order" (1994, 203). Mud threatens boundaries. It makes trouble. Imagined as a borderland, it might be understood as a "vague and undetermined space ... in a constant state of transition" (Anzaldúa 2012, 25). Here, it is not the boundary breaking that threatens, but the fact that mud in its basic composition resists the very notion of boundaries; this resistance to form is visceral and embodied, and it provokes equally embodied responses.

Moving beyond Ahmed's notion of stickiness as encounter, we might consider mud itself as lacking integrity. Already a product of stickiness, mud is itself in a process of continual resurfacing. Sediment and water continuously interact with one another, constantly churning and moving together to create the substance we know as mud. Mud is vibrant matter (Bennett 2010). A substance that drags its histories along, it carries within itself not only the sands that mark its journeys, but also human sediments: the storied bones, the fishnets, the plastics, the detritus of lives lived and lost. Mud is thus not a single substance, but a conglomeration, a constellation, an assemblage of substances; in its constant movement, it articulates the *terra infirma* (Rogoff 2000) of unstable, shifting geographies, gathering histories into itself even as the sediment swirls through the water, resurfacing itself with every new layer of sedimentation. If we are all watery, as Neimanis (2012, 2013, 2017) argues, then we are also all muddy, our sticky surfaces and glutinous clingings inhering in our very beings.

But if conventional definitions locate mud as a site of filth, disorder, pollution, and trouble, then what of the corporeal pleasures of mud? What of that feeling of toes squelching and squirching in cool mud on a hot summer's day? What of the damp, moist earth that gardeners work between their fingers? What of the visceral pleasures and delights of formlessness, that intimate stickiness that we embrace, long for, desire? Can we consider mud as a provocation to intimacy (Berlant 2000)? As a form of resistance, a productive site of imagination, inspiration? Can we play with mud differently?

If mud has, as a foundational quality, opacity—rendering things darker, inaccessible, and sticky—it is also tactile and malleable; it is a formlessness that can be reshaped in any number of ways. So might we consider mud as a space of possibility and transformation (Howitt 2001, 240). Mud, here, is not shameful, dark, or disgusting; rather, it is Cixous' wound: generative, productive, gestational (Cixous 1998, xiv).

Playing with mud must attend to mud in all of its forms. Mud is intersected with multiple meanings. It is indeed infested and polluted—a space of horror and disgust—but it is also imaginative, tactile, and redemptive. Mudplay must acknowledge mud's intentionality: its constant resurfacing, its continual reimagining, reinventing, and reshaping. Mud is the layering of past and present; it is both sedimentation and fragmentation. Within itself, mud is continually revising and reinventing itself, shoring itself up even as it erodes itself. Playing with mud is an act of creation, the making of mud with and through others. Mudplay is about embracing formlessness, engaging with the sticky; it is about living our hauntings and accessing our futures through our pasts.

An evocation of—or invocation to—mud, in its constant oozing, may allow us to consider mud as a metaphor for movement and migration; it is a space of and for transition. The surfacing and resurfacing intentionality of mud evokes the dense stickiness that results when peoples move around, encounter, meet, and struggle. Mud as a product of erosion, meanwhile, reminds us that geographies are always unstable at the water's edge (Carter 2008; see also Chap. 10, later in this volume). As an undoing—a gnawing away at an older order—mud reveals stories to us. At the same time, it shows us that we can tell new stories.

Perhaps, then, we might return to the scandalous nature of mud. Mud is about deception, about fraud, about truths that are not what they seem. Mud clouds, obscuring 'facts' while simultaneously revealing the fictions on which those facts were founded. Playing with mud, then, is about fraud—about scandal, about trouble. It is about what happens at the bottom, with the dregs. It is about challenging boundaries once thought determined, and showing the gaps and silences within them.

Mud, as vibrant matter at the water's edge, exists only through a layering of histories, the murky swirling of earth with water, past with present. Always shifting and changing, it exists only in the plural; it can never be reduced to a single element. Both haunted and haunting, mud can function as a site of memory and remembering. In its continual shifting, it can also enable a transcorporeal (Alaimo 2008) politics of belonging, a model for living better together in an ever-eroding, ever-shifting, constantly resurfacing world.

[SB]

References

Ahmed, Sara. 2004. *The cultural politics of emotion*. New York: Routledge.

Alaimo, Stacy. 2008. Trans-corporeal feminisms and the ethical space of nature. In *Material feminisms*, ed. Stacy Alaimo and Susan Hekman, 237–264. Bloomington and Indianapolis: Indiana University Press.

Anzaldúa, Gloria. 2012. *Borderlands/la frontera: The new mestiza*. 4th ed. San Francisco: Aunt Lute Books.

Bennett, Jane. 2010. *Vibrant matter: A political ecology of things*. Durham: Duke University Press.

Berlant, Lauren, ed. 2000. *Intimacy*. Chicago and London: University of Chicago Press.

Carter, Paul. 2008. *Dark writing: Geography, performance, design*. Honolulu: University of Hawaii Press.

Cixous, Hélène. 1998. *Stigmata: Escaping texts*. New York: Routledge.

Douglas, Mary. 1969. *Purity and danger: An analysis of concepts of pollution and taboo*. 2nd ed. London: Routledge and Kegan Paul.

Gordon, Avery. 1997. *Ghostly matters: Haunting and the sociological imagination*. Minneapolis: University of Minnesota Press.

Grosz, Elizabeth A. 1994. *Volatile bodies: Toward a corporeal feminism*. Bloomington: Indiana University Press.

Howitt, Richie. 2001. Frontiers, borders, edges: Liminal challenges to the hegemony of exclusion. *Australian Geographical Studies* 39 (2): 233–245. https://doi.org/10.1111/1467-8470.00142.

Kristeva, Julia. 1982. *Powers of horror: An essay on abjection*. Trans. Leon S. Roudiez. New York: Columbia University Press.

McKenzie, Kirsten. 2005. *Scandal in the colonies: Sydney and Cape Town, 1820–1850*. Carlton: Melbourne University Press.

mud, n.1. OED Online. 2017, March. Oxford University Press. http://www.oed.com.qe2a-proxy.mun.ca/view/Entry/123226?rskey=40weRy&result=1. Accessed 6 June 2017.

Neimanis, Astrida. 2012. Hydrofeminism: Or, on becoming a body of water. In *Undutiful daughters: New directions in feminist thought and practice*, ed. Henriette Gunkel, Chrysanthi Nigianni, and Fanny Soderback, 96–115. New York: Palgrave Macmillan.

———. 2013. Feminist subjectivity, watered. *Feminist Review* 103: 23–31.

———. 2017. *Bodies of water: Posthuman feminist phenomenology*. London: Bloomsbury Academic.

Rogoff, Irit. 2000. *Terra infirma: Geography's visual culture*. London and New York: Routledge.

Tuana, Nancy. 2008. Viscous porosity: Witnessing Katrina. In *Material feminisms*, ed. Stacy Alaimo and Susan Hekman, 188–213. Bloomington: Indiana University Press.

Tuck, Eve, and C. Ree. 2013. A glossary of haunting. In *Handbook of autoethnography*, ed. Stacey Holman Jones, Tony E. Adams, and Carolyn Ellis, 639–658. Walnut Grove: Left Coast Press.

CHAPTER 6

Futures: Unfrozen

Abstract From rough and solid slabs, to pans and bergs, ice is a key marker of Newfoundland identity, an intimate point of encounter between the human and the more-than-human. But what will ice mean—and what will Newfoundland identity mean—in the face of ongoing climate change? If ice pans mark Newfoundlanders' relationships with physical and political landscapes, then what happens when the ice is gone? This essay suggests that thinking through embodied and emotional geographies about our frozen selves can enable us to live differently with and through ice.

Keywords Ice • Emotional geographies • Embodied identity • Climate change • Newfoundland

Over a decade ago in spring, I found myself amidst a group of rural children leaping from one ice pan to the next across the harbour near my home. In this game known as copy-panning, one child acts as a leader across floating slabs of ice, and a string of other children follow, one by one. As the weight of my body bore down on the fragile floe for a few seconds at a time, saltwater flooded around my feet and frigid rushes moved through me. The water below was cold and black, and there was no bottom in sight. Why were we fooling around like that? What was it about the risk that drew us in? My mother's voice popped in my head, yelling: "Stay

© The Author(s) 2018
S. Boon et al., *Autoethnography and Feminist Theory at the Water's Edge*, https://doi.org/10.1007/978-3-319-90829-8_6

clear of the wharf, and don't go out on the ice!" It wasn't the first time I'd heard her say this; I had paid no mind to her instructions before, even though she'd shared stories about young children in my hometown drowning while jumping across the pans.

Writing about my emotive relations to sea ice illustrates the impact of the ocean in my life as a rural islander. I have formed many stories with sea ice. Its presence as a wintry companion has forever changed me, chilled me. Each year as I await its return, I wonder whether it has been frozen afresh, or drifted from the ancient Arctic. I have never been afraid of ice, and perhaps I am lucky. I haven't lost anything to it; rather ice has given me so much. What can I offer it? How can I hold on to it, be frozen into it?

Studying Newfoundland literature, Caitlin Charman (2010) notes that there is a delicate interplay between loss, Newfoundland identity, and the ocean. Indeed, classic Newfoundland texts have offered visual depictions of the treacherous natures of sea ice (Brown and Horwood 1972; Morgan 1992). At times, ice is a frightening liminal space upon which lives become endangered; the frozen surface of the sea is a site of loss. Ice constricts, cracks, and covers, but it can also be etched upon. Interactions between ice and its surroundings shape its place in ethno-ecologies.

I join a group of Newfoundland and Labrador writers who have given ice a literary presence as a tool for navigation, a frozen actant that helps us negotiate our relations to the environment (Goudie 1973; Johnston 1998; Kavanagah 1996). Islanders and Labradorians are affected by ice in diverse ways. In Labrador, ice is an Indigenous lifeline (Albeck-Ripka 2017). Vital on both spiritual and material grounds, it shapes worldviews, connects communities, and offers access to food and resources. Yet no matter the significance of the frozen substance, a troubling decline in Labrador sea ice continues to affect the First peoples of this province.

On the island, rough ice packs itself into harbours and grounds at the shoreline, collecting traces of soil and sea life. Rough ice is supposed to last for a season; it is solid and should break apart slowly. Pans of ice, however, are nomadic storytellers (Braidotti 2014). They shift and dance on the water, moving in and out of fluid spaces almost at will. Unfortunately, while ice pans bring aesthetic pleasures and games of risk, and rough ice brings islanders the economic opportunities of the seal fishery, today their presence is fleeting. Newfoundlanders must recognize this. Forming affective, embodied connections with ice, I highlight the need to conceptualize the frozen substance in terms of loss. Because ice preserves memories and has a critical ecological voice (Sörlin 2017), what might happen to rural stories and subjectivities connected to—and frozen in—icescapes as climate change continues to affect Newfoundland and Labrador? The work of anthropologists, geographers, environmental historians, and health researchers has illustrated complex epistemological, political, and ethno-ecological relations to ice (Bravo 2009; Cunsolo Willox 2012; Cruikshank 2005; Ford et al. 2014; Sörlin 2017; Steinberg and Kristoffersen 2017). Ashlee Cunsolo Willox has noted how climate change and melting sea ice in Labrador has had detrimental health effects for Inuit communities (2012). Issues of isolation and accessibility, as well as a threatened food supply, are facilitated by the loss of ice. Ultimately, as sea ice melts, communities, cultural identities, and everyday lives are threatened (Ford et al. 2014).

As Stacy Alaimo argues, the human is inseparable from the more-than-human (2010, 2). Vicki Hallett's research on Newfoundland masculinities (2016a) and decolonial life writing practices (2016b) takes up this notion as she explores the vernacular metaphysics and poetics of living in a province where saltwater is a vital substance that runs through our veins (2016b, 316). Further, the loss of sea ice problematizes the romanticized relations to water by which islanders are discursively produced (see Chap. 17). Melting ice is a troubling occurrence, and like Alaimo (2012), I believe that collaborative artistic, scientific, and theoretical contributions will be necessary to think about wet and slippery futures for Newfoundlanders.

In a memory—frozen—I catch a glimpse of my own surroundings at the border between solid and liquid. As I witness spatial and elemental boundaries spilling into and over one another, I see trans-temporal inscriptions carved in rock by the feelers of waves and sea ice: the way that they have played with Newfoundland's edges, forming rugged lines where land touches water in bursts, and at places in the sides of cliffs where that touching never stops, smooth surfaces like innocent skin from continuous erosion (Hallett 2010; see also Chap. 10, later in this volume). I know what water feels like, but how does water feel? Does water have its own longings? As Deborah Bird Rose asks, "what is water's own living presence" (2007, 12)?

With a swift jump, I landed on a small ice pan, but before I could move to the next, it cracked. In a split second, the cold water around my feet rushed up, pouring into my boots, and then my feet went numb. Before I knew it, I was beneath the surface, yanked under by the weight of my soaked snowsuit. Dazed and flailing in the wet, I was pulled back up on to a sheet of solid ice by a few of the other children, where I caught my breath and wrung as much water as I could out of my clothes to feel less heavy. The kids made sure I was all right, and walked me home to be scolded by my parents. And when I was dry and warm again, I laughed about the whole thing. Shivering after the shock, covered in goosebumps, I had been changed. I would never be the same. I would realize that ice was something more than an object. It was dangerous, playful, beautiful. It traveled, it glistened, it captivated me.

Surrounded by ice pans and soaked in frigid water, I call for Newfoundlanders and Labradorians, especially those of us who are settlers, to re/think our textured relations to the environment. I believe that frozen imagery of, and affective turns toward, touching and feeling (Kosofsky Sedgwick 2003) can reshape the way we live with the more-than-human. We need ecological intimacy. Continuously learning as I think and write about my relations to the environment, I become more aware of my intra-active touching (Barad 2007)—surface to surface—with ice. I become frozen for short moments and the cold becomes me (see Chap. 3). Does it feel what I feel? Does it melt into the water or drift beyond with stories of my life? As a kid, I would break off pieces of ice that grounded on the beach and crunch them up in my mouth. I am still affected by the taste of ice so ancient, so clear. I think about my communication with ice: my jumping on to, my chipping away at, my tasting of, my travels across, ice. How would I understand my identity as an islander without it? How could we navigate a future on the island without the icescapes into which our selves are frozen?

Owain Jones suggests that "each spatialized, felt, moment or sequence of the now-being-laid-down is … mapped into our bodies and minds to become a vast store of past geographies which shape who we are" (2005, 206). As an islander and a young woman raised alongside the ocean, I feel environmental changes most frequently through matter-realist (Braidotti 2014) touches at the shoreline. I watch boats of fisherfolk come and go, see garbage and waste thrown into the ocean wash back to land, and watch rough ice pack into the harbour. I am frozen in place by the ice. It calls me out and I don't care if it cracks. I trust it. I want that rush. If New World Island, my island-within-an-island home, wasn't connected to the mainland by a causeway, I would spend months isolated and entrapped by rough ice. My body would only know rough ice.

Eventually, as I play near the shoreline, ice breaks apart and drifts out of the harbour. In time, and by chance, I will see icebergs come and ground on the ocean floor. Alive even in their iciness, they are constantly changing, their contours melting in the spring sun, their bodies turning to fragments over a short while. I see ice pans undulate, dance, on the water. They invite me to play, to change form. I become more-than-human. At times I am solid, then liquid. I float on top. Then I am in, and I am water. I splash, I melt, I freeze.

To form a wet epistemology with sea ice in Newfoundland and Labrador is to be a nomad, a border crosser, a subject becoming-with water and ice at a number of various cultural, ecological, ethnic and geographic shore-lines (Braidotti 2002, 2014; Wright 2014). Indeed, shorelines are sites "of exchange rather than a boundary between two distinct spaces" (Steinberg and Kristoffersen 2017, 628). Interchanging contact zones for thinking about icy nature-cultures (Carter 1999; Pratt 2002), shorelines encourage us to simultaneously feel, live and theorize with borders and phase transitions (see Chap. 5). They also signify a mixture of environmental relations between future and past, earth and ocean, First peoples and settlers.

Ethno-ecological relations with sea ice in Newfoundland and Labrador help visualize a critical relationship between the environment and the diverse needs, desires, and subjectivities of Indigenous and settler communities across our provincial spaces. In this essay, my melting and mourning with ice allows me to think-with climate change on embodied and emotive terms (Cunsolo Willox 2012). As I seek out a wet epistemology that is slippery and melting away, I wonder if thinking through and using water, as Stacy Alaimo (2012) and Astrida Neimanis (2013, 2017) believe, is truly the way to a better future for all lives on Earth. What might a frozen approach to thinking with water look like? If I imagine these few paragraphs, like ice pans, drifting with and rubbing against one another—perhaps even breaking off—what can I learn about my place in the icescapes of Newfoundland and Labrador?

[DJ]

REFERENCES

Alaimo, Stacy. 2010. *Bodily natures: Science, environment, and the material self.* Bloomington: Indiana University Press.

———. 2012. Sustainable this, sustainable that: New materialisms, posthumanism, and unknown futures. *PMLA: Publications of the Modern Language Association of America* 127 (3): 558–564. https://doi.org/10.1632/pmla.2012.127.3.558.

Albeck-Ripka, Livia. 2017. Why lost ice means lost hope for an Inuit village. *New York Times*. https://www.nytimes.com/interactive/2017/11/25/climate/arctic-climate-change.html. Accessed 20 Mar 2018.

Barad, Karen. 2007. *Meeting the universe halfway: Quantum physics and the entanglement of matter and meaning*. Durham, NC: Duke University Press.

Braidotti, Rosi. 2002. *Metamorphoses: Towards a materialist theory of becoming*. Cambridge: Polity Press.

———. 2014. Writing as a nomadic subject. *Comparative Critical Studies* 11 (2–3): 163–184. https://doi.org/10.3366/ccs.2014.0122.

Bravo, Michael. 2009. Sea ice mapping: Ontology, mechanics and human rights at the ice floe edge. In *High places: Cultural geographies of mountains, ice and science*, ed. Denis Cosgrove and Veronica Della Dora, 162–177. London: I.B. Tauris.

Brown, Cassie, and Harold Horwood. 1972. *Death on the ice: The great Newfoundland sealing disaster of 1914*. Toronto: Doubleday.

Carter, Paul. 1999. Dark with excess of bright: Mapping the coastlines of knowledge. In *Mappings*, ed. Denis Cosgrove, 125–147. London: Reaktion.

Charman, Caitlin. 2010. A littoral place: Loss and environment in contemporary Newfoundland fiction. PhD dissertation. Queen's University.

Cruikshank, Julie. 2005. *Do glaciers speak? Local knowledge, colonial encounters, and social imagination*. Vancouver: UBC Press.

Cunsolo Willox, Ashlee. 2012. Climate change as the work of mourning. *Ethics & The Environment* 17 (2): 137–164.

Ford, James D., et al. 2014. Adapting to the effects of climate change on Inuit health. *American Journal of Public Health* 104 (S3): e9–e17. https://doi.org/10.2105/AJPH.2013.301724.

Goudie, Elizabeth. 1973. *Woman of labrador*. Toronto: Peter Martin Associates.

Hallett, Vicki. 2010. Continuous erosion: Place and identity in the lives of Newfoundland women. In *Despite this loss: Essays on culture, memory and identity in Newfoundland and Labrador*, ed. Ursula A. Kelly and Elizabeth Yeoman, 74–91. St. John's: ISER Books.

———. 2016a. Cold water cowboys and Newfoundland masculinity. *Acadiensis*. https://acadiensis.wordpress.com/2016/06/13/cold-water-cowboys-and-newfoundland-masculinity. Accessed 18 Mar 2018.

———. 2016b. Fluid possibilities: Theorizing life writing at the confluence of decolonial and post-colonial approaches in Newfoundland and Labrador. *Newfoundland and Labrador Studies* 31 (2): 316–328.

Johnston, Wayne. 1998. *The colony of unrequited dreams*. Toronto: Knopf.

Jones, Owain. 2005. An ecology of emotion, memory, self and landscape. In *Emotional geographies*, ed. Joyce Davidson, Liz Bondi, and Mick Smith, 205–218. Aldershot: Ashgate.

Kavanagah, Peter. 1996. *Gaff topsails*. Toronto: Viking.

Morgan, Bernice. 1992. *Random passage*. St. John's: Breakwater Books.

Neimanis, Astrida. 2013. Feminist subjectivity, watered. *Feminist Review* 103: 23–31. https://doi.org/10.1057/fr.2012.25.

———. 2017. *Bodies of water: Posthuman feminist phenomenology*. Sydney: Bloomsbury.

Pratt, Mary Louise. 2002. The arts of the contact zone. In *Ways of reading: An anthology for writers*, ed. David Bartholomae and Anthony Petrosky, 604–662. Boston: Bedford-St. Martin's.

Rose, Deborah Bird. 2007. Justice and longing. In *Fresh water: New perspectives on water in Australia*, ed. Emily Potter, Alison Mackinnon, Stephen McKenzie, and Jennifer McKay, 8–20. Melbourne: Melbourne University Publishing.

Sedgwick, Eve Kosofsky. 2003. *Touching feeling: Affect, pedagogy, performativity*. Durham and London: Duke University Press.

Sörlin, Sverker. 2017. Do glaciers speak?: The political aesthetics of vo/ice. In *Methodological challenges in nature-culture and environmental history research*, ed. Jocelyn Thorpe, Stephanie Rutherford, and L. Anders Sandberg, 13–30. New York: Routledge.

Steinberg, Philip, and Berit Kristoffersen. 2017. "The ice edge is lost... nature moved it": Mapping ice as state practice in the Canadian and Norwegian North. *Transactions of the Institute of British Geographers* 42 (4): 625–641. https://doi.org/10.1111/tran.12184.

Wright, Kate. 2014. Becoming-with: Living lexicon for the environmental humanities. *Environmental Humanities* 5: 277–281. https://doi.org/10.1215/22011919-3615514.

PART II

Geographies

CHAPTER 7

Land: Landscape

Abstract Framed around family vacations with a geographer parent, this essay considers the meanings of landscapes. Scientific understandings suggest that land is measurable; sensuous geographies, however, offer a different way in. Drawing on the work of Katherine McKittrick, bell hooks, and Leanne Betasamosake Simpson, as well as childhood engagements with the micro-geographies of plant life in Newfoundland, this chapter asserts a need to work closely and intimately with the land, tuning in to the multiplicity of our senses to help reveal the landscape as an assemblage of smaller things continually and complexly interconnected.

Keywords Landscape • Poetics • Pedagogy • Assemblage

"Can you stand there for scale?" As I looked at an old photo of myself from a family vacation—scowling and with my arms firmly crossed—standing in front of a barren valley in Drumheller, Alberta, I couldn't help but laugh. I could hear my mother's voice, her wheedling request. My mother, a geographer, loved taking pictures of unique landscapes, and I was regularly called on to step into the photo for scale. I usually complied, but I always resented it. It wasn't that I didn't like having my picture taken. Rather, my resentment stemmed from the nature of my mother's request. If I had just been asked to stand in front of the camera, for myself and not for scale, I would have happily replaced my scowl with a smile. Standing

© The Author(s) 2018
S. Boon et al., *Autoethnography and Feminist Theory at the Water's Edge*, https://doi.org/10.1007/978-3-319-90829-8_7

for scale made me feel like I was nothing more than a tool, something necessary to measure the land behind me. Instead of being a part of the picture—part of the landscape that so fascinated my mother—I was made to feel separate, disconnected from the scenery around me. Perhaps, then, my peevish pose was just a comically feeble attempt at injecting some personality—some feeling—into the photograph.

According to Gillian Rose "seeing and knowing are often conflated" (1993, 86). But can we truly understand landscapes solely through the visual (see also Chaps. 6 and 9)? What might we learn from the land if we look beyond the ocular frame? Due to the centrality of fieldwork in geography, where fieldwork primarily relies on looking, the range of the observer's vision often becomes assumed as full knowledge (Rose 1993, 86; Dowler et al. 2005, 3). But Yi-Fu Tuan admits that while sight is "our most active cognitive sense," it is also the "least emotional" (1984, 8; see also Sedgwick 2003). As he explains, "We can see only what is in front; we necessarily stand at the margin of our own visual field. All objects in it, no matter how close, still seem 'out there'" (Tuan 1984, 8). In terms of the study of landscape, the dominance of vision essentially "distances us from the landscape," both physically and psychologically (Porteous 1990, 5; see also Tuan 1984, 8; Wylie 2007). However, if geography is, at its heart, the study of landscape, then what really lies at the heart of landscapes (Porteous 1990, 3)? Can we generate knowledge of the land beyond looking? What can we learn if we consider the sensuous composition of the land (Rodaway 1994)?

While my mother's interest in the more scientific notions of land may have sparked my critical stance on "standing for scale" as a child, her critical lenses also shaped how I understood the landscape. She was the one who taught me to look *beyond* just looking at the landscape. More specifically, she encouraged me to "have fun with plants," to explore—through touch, taste, smell, sound—the details that actually make a landscape. I remember these moments without a camera, and without the calculated pose—these moments where I saw the landscape through an intimate interaction with the land itself—with much more fondness.

Exploring the components that made up a landscape provided a more thorough and memorable learning experience for me. While Drumheller's eerie lunar landscape remained remote and untouchable, here, in Newfoundland, I learned about carnivorous pitcher plants by feeling the hairs within the pitchers: smooth as my fingers followed them downward, and rough as they resisted the upward pull of my finger. I explored, too, the tastes of the land as my family and I foraged Newfoundland's fields for blueberries in late summer. Often, I would reward myself for filling a bucket by eating a handful of those tiny, sweet berries straight from the bushes. While hiking Newfoundland's trails, I also learned about both the cultural and physical influences upon landscapes through wildflowers. My mother taught me which flowers I could pick and tie into my ponytail, but also pointed out those that were too rare for my prying fingers to pluck from the ground. Other times, the painful scratching of thistles and rose bushes against my legs forced me to learn about the anatomy—and autonomy—of flora the hard way. Ultimately, these affective journeys through the land taught me that just as humans shape the land, so too, does the land shape us (Bennett 2010; Neimanis and Walker 2014; see also Anderson 1952; Schiebinger 2005).

Despite the petulance that marked my Drumheller pose, there is nothing inherently wrong with attention to scale. However, it can become problematic when we rely on an assumption of scale as a value neutral, objective measurement. After all, geographic discourse is not always objective; there is always a human behind the scale, and a hand behind the camera. Marsha Weisiger reminds us that scale is dependent upon our perception; the ways in which we read the land rely on—and change with—our point of view (2017, 38). Black feminist geographies in particular have done much to break this illusion of objectivity. For example, historical examinations of slave auction blocks reveal how scale has historically marginalized black bodies as "distinct" and "radically different" from white bodies (McKittrick 2006, 75, 82). As Katherine McKittrick writes, "the poetics of landscape are utilized to not only humanize the point of sale, but exploit the inherent weaknesses of scale" (2006, 79). Scale here is an indication of the powerful social dimensions of place, a tool with which to contain bodies and experiences within the politically-produced boundaries of space (McKittrick 2006, 83). Scale, therefore comes to represent both the "oppressive and emancipatory possibilities of space" (Smith, qtd. in McKittrick 2006, 83). As a result, despite any intentions to the contrary, scale cannot be defined, nor confined, outside of the social context within which it exists. In a way, these perspectives of space and scale are much like the silencing attempts of colonialism upon language (see Chap. 14).

However, despite colonial attempts at control, either through scale or silence, we can still find resistance from *within*, from bodies claiming a space of their own. Much like my own desire to have "fun with plants," bell hooks writes of the significance of "touching the earth" (2009, 34). Fondly recounting her childhood days of playing in the Kentucky soil, she suggests that, "when we love the earth, we are able to love ourselves more fully" (hooks 2009, 34; see also Chap. 3). While identifying often overlooked connections between land, history, and bodies, hooks notes the particular significance of each upon African and Native American peoples' sense of place and identity (hooks 2009, 36; see also Philip 1997). Here, the recollection of ancestral legacies of the land becomes a step towards the reclamation of well-being, both for the self and the earth (hooks 2009, 40).

Similarly, attention to Traditional Knowledge can help us expand our land-based experiences and education (Simpson 2014). According to Leanne Betasamosake Simpson, stories work to reclaim "land as pedagogy" (2014, 1). She tells a traditional Michi Saagiig Nishnaabeg story of a young girl, Kwezens, who learns how to make maple syrup by observing and listening to the land (2014, 2–5). By watching the actions of a squirrel, not only does Kwezens learn a new skill, but she also learns about compassion and understanding, and demonstrates creativity and conceptual thought (Simpson 2014, 6). Here, "land, aki, is both context and process," whereby "coming to know is the pursuit of whole body intelligence" (Simpson 2014, 7). Thus, intimacy and intelligence, story and theory, become interconnected in the process of learning, and in the process of land. For Simpson, as for hooks, reflecting on ancestral legacies and stories becomes an opportunity to learn not only of the past, but of the possibility of our presents and futures. Intimacy with the land—through touch, spirituality, and emotion—helps individuals connect not only to nature, but to themselves and their communities (Simpson 2014, 7; see also Million 2009).

While much geographic research still relies on conventional approaches, there has been a dynamic turn towards Indigenous ways of knowing to broaden and enrich the discipline. For example, some geographers are now working with Indigenous communities to study climate change, where Inuit are able to determine changes in ice thickness by *listening* to it ("As ice thins underfoot" 2018; see also Chap. 6, earlier in this volume). By merging more traditional geographic methods with traditional Inuit knowledge, learning goes beyond the visual. And if we learn to listen, we might just realize what *can* speak (Cruikshank 2005; Jackson and Fannin 2011; Sörlin 2017). Not only does bridging the gap between Indigenous and Western ways of knowing expand our sensorial and pedagogical potential, it also challenges settler colonial perceptions of the land, a step towards the actual decolonization of land (Metallic 2017, 126; Simpson 2014, 23).

Engaging with the land has helped me learn about the wider relationship between human and nature, as well as the contentious 'divide' between them, and the bridges we can build through dynamic and subjective understanding (Barad 2012; Buttimer 1984, 56; Jackson and Fannin 2011; Rodaway 1994). In a way, tuning in to the multiplicity of our senses helps reveal what a landscape really is: a collection of smaller things, of plants and animals—of the more-than-human—not in isolation from a human behind a camera (or in my case, in front of it), but as continually and complexly interconnected (Bennett 2010). If we move beyond the idea of landscape as something 'over there,' and instead as something in which we reside, we can begin to see landscapes not as a mythical Other, but as a "lifeworld," a world in which we live, not just a scene to behold (Wylie 2007, 149; see also Chap. 1). If we reach our hands beyond the lens—to reach out and touch—we might just realize that land does not merely surround us. Land shapes us. Perhaps then we will begin to see landscapes as not only pictures, but as sensuous, vibrant experiences (Bennett 2010; Buttimer 1984, 60).

[LB]

REFERENCES

Anderson, Edgar. 1952. *Plants, man and life*. Berkeley and Los Angeles: University of California Press.

As ice thins underfoot, technology is combining with traditional Inuit knowledge to save lives. 2018. *CBC Radio: The Current*. http://www.cbc.ca/radio/thecurrent/the-current-for-january-04-2018-1.4471709/as-ice-thins-underfoot-technology-is-combining-with-traditional-inuit-knowledge-to-save-lives-1.4472915. Accessed 17 Feb 2018.

Barad, Karen. 2012. On touching: The inhuman that therefore I am. *Differences: A Journal of Feminist Cultural Studies* 23 (3): 206–223. https://doi.org/10.1215/10407391-1892943.

Bennett, Jane. 2010. *Vibrant matter: A political ecology of things*. Durham: Duke University Press.

Buttimer, Anne. 1984. Musing on helicon: Root metaphors and geography. In *Place: Experience and symbol*, ed. Miles Richardson, 55–62. Baton Rouge: Geoscience Publications, Dept. of Geography and Anthropology, Louisiana State University.

Cruikshank, Julie. 2005. *Do glaciers listen?: Local knowledge, colonial encounters, and social imagination*. Vancouver: UBC Press.

Dowler, Lorraine, Josephine Carubia, and Bonj Szczygiel. 2005. Introduction: Renegotiating morality and space. In *Gender and landscape: Renegotiating morality and space*, ed. Lorraine Dowler, Josephine Carubia, and Bonj Szczygiel, 1–15. New York: Routledge.

hooks, bell. 2009. *Belonging: A culture of place*. New York and London: Routledge.

Jackson, Mark, and Maria Fannin. 2011. Letting geography fall where it may— Aerographies address the elemental. *Environment and Planning D: Society and Space* 29: 435–444. https://doi.org/10.1068/d2903ed.

McKittrick, Katherine. 2006. *Demonic grounds: Black women and the cartographies of struggle*. Minneapolis: University of Minnesota Press.

Metallic, Fred. 2017. Decolonizing intellectual traditions: Conducting research and telling our stories in a 'Mi'gmaq way'. In *Methodological challenges in nature-culture and environmental history research*, ed. Jocelyn Thorpe, Stephanie Rutherford, and L. Anders Sandberg, 120–130. New York: Routledge.

Million, Dian. 2009. Felt theory: An Indigenous feminist approach to affect and history. *Wicazo Sa Review* 24 (2): 53–76. https://doi.org/10.1353/wic.0.0043.

Neimanis, Astrida, and Rachel Loewen Walker. 2014. Weathering: Climate change and the "thick time" of transcorporeality. *Hypatia* 29 (3): 558–575. https://doi.org/10.1111/hypa.12064.

Philip, M. NourbeSe. 1997. Dis/Place: The space between. In *A genealogy of resistance—And other essays*, 74–112. Toronto: Mercury Press.

Porteous, J. Douglas. 1990. *Landscapes of the mind: Worlds of sense and metaphor*. Toronto: University of Toronto Press.

Rodaway, Paul. 1994. *Sensuous geographies: Body, sense and place*. London and New York: Routledge.

Rose, Gillian. 1993. *Feminism and geography: The limits of geographical knowledge*. Minneapolis: University of Minnesota Press.

Schiebinger, Londa. 2005. Agnotology and exotic abortifacients: The cultural production of ignorance in the eighteenth-century Atlantic world. *Proceedings of the American Philosophical Society* 149 (3): 316–343.

Sedgwick, Eve Kosofsky. 2003. *Touching feeling: Affect, pedagogy, performativity*. Durham: Duke University Press.

Simpson, Leanne Betasamosake. 2014. Land as pedagogy: Nishnaabeg intelligence and rebellious transformation. *Decolonization: Indigeneity, Education & Society* 3 (3): 1–25.

Sörlin, Sverker. 2017. Do glaciers speak?: The political aesthetic of vo/ice. In *Methodological challenges in nature-culture and environmental history research*, ed. Jocelyn Thorpe, Stephanie Rutherford, and L. Anders Sandberg, 13–30. New York: Routledge.

Tuan, Yi-Fu. 1984. In place, out of place. In *Place: Experience and symbol*, ed. Miles Richardson, 3–10. Baton Rouge: Geoscience Publications, Dept. of Geography and Anthropology, Louisiana State University.

Weisiger, Marsha. 2017. Experiencing Earth art: Or, lessons from reading the landscape. In *Methodological challenges in nature-culture and environmental history research*, ed. Jocelyn Thorpe, Stephanie Rutherford, and L. Anders Sandberg, 31–42. New York: Routledge.

Wylie, John. 2007. *Landscape*. New York: Routledge.

CHAPTER 8

Water: Flooding Memory

Abstract This chapter takes up notions of the fluid, which have long been central to feminist theorizing, in order to consider the memory of water. Locating water as sentient; that is, alive with its own potentiality, and drawing on the work of Astrida Neimanis, Sara Ahmed, Nancy Tuana, and Deborah Bird Rose, among others, it asks how humans might better think with and through water.

Keywords Memory • Water • Seepage • Bodies

In an essay entitled "The site of memory," Toni Morrison (1995) meditates on the memory of water. "You know," she writes, "they straightened out the Mississippi River in places, to make room for houses and livable acreage. Occasionally the river floods these places. 'Floods' is the word they use, but in fact it is not flooding; it is remembering. Remembering where it used to be. All water has a perfect memory and is forever trying to get back to where it was" (1995, 98–9). Water, Morrison suggests here, has stories to tell. It tells them not in words, but in the way that it sculpts and shapes the landscape.

River stories trace paths across the landscapes I've called home. Some rivers rush forward, carving straight lines across fields or between rocks. Others snake around. Meandering through the landscape, they deposit layers of silt at every corner, snaking their stories through soil and mud. As

© The Author(s) 2018
S. Boon et al., *Autoethnography and Feminist Theory at the Water's Edge*, https://doi.org/10.1007/978-3-319-90829-8_8

a child, I'd peer out over the landscape looking for hints of the river's histories, searching for the memory of water. Imagine, then, my delight when I recently discovered—entirely by accident—Harold Fisk's map of the Mississippi River (1944). Here, in a tangle of coloured ribbons threading together in yellow, green, pink, red, and blue, I could follow the river's changing courses over time, tracing the ghostly stories embedded in a now haunted landscape. In his map, Fisk, like Morrison, recognized the intentionality of the river, its agency, its living essence.

What can we learn from water? How might an engagement with water inform our politics, our daily living, our selves? In a 2013 article, Astrida Neimanis proposes a "watered" form of feminist subjectivity, one that attends not only to human concerns, but also to ethical engagements with the nonhuman. Extending feminist posthumanist conversations initiated by such thinkers as Donna Haraway and Rosi Braidotti, she observes that "we are bodies of water, but we also reside within and as part of a fragile global hydrocommons, where water—the lifeblood of humans and all other bodies on this planet—is increasingly contaminated, commodified and dangerously reorganized" (2013, 27). As Elspeth Probyn (2016) would argue, we are deeply entangled with the more-than-human, our bodies fishy, watery, queer (see also Chaps. 2 and 3). But what does it mean to imagine ourselves as water bodies? How might our approach to politics change if we think of ourselves through our relationships with the more-than-human, rather than against them? What new possibilities might emerge?

I've long been fascinated by the liquid, the fluid, the stuff that resists borders, flows beyond them, and renders them obsolete. The fluid or liquid is not unique to posthumanist theorizing, nor is it necessarily new to feminist theorizing. Many other thinkers, too, have explored the productive potential of the fluid. Hélène Cixous (1976), for example, starts with the "white ink" of the lactating maternal body as a source for a utopian feminist imaginary. In her wake, numerous other thinkers, among them Alison Bartlett (2005; see also Shaw and Bartlett 2010), Quinn Eades (2015), Fiona Giles (2002, 2004, 2005), Robyn Longhurst (2001, 2008), Margrit Shildrick (1997), and Iris Marion Young (2005) have taken up, extended, expanded, and explored these notions. Most visceral, perhaps, has been Julia Kristeva who, in *Powers of horror*, imagines the fluid as threat locating it as a point of horror: vomit, sewage, and pus. The site of abjection, the fluid undermines the authority of the self even as it confirms it: "I expel *myself*, I spit *myself* out, I abject *myself* within the same motion through which 'I' claim to establish *myself*" (1982, 3; italics original).

The fluid, in these works, is resistant, uncontainable, and unknowable. Within our current political order, the fluid cannot be theorized; it remains outside of structures of knowledge. The fluid is the feminine, the unruly, the disruptive. Alternately emancipatory and liberatory, or abject and polluting, the fluid is that which resists and refuses normative structures, that which cannot be defined. Elizabeth Grosz, in her now foundational *Volatile bodies: Towards a corporeal feminism*, suggests that "women's corporeality is inscribed in a mode of seepage" (1994, 203), arguing that in the Western philosophical, political, and social imaginary, women are represented as "leaky," "formless," "uncontrollable," and as such, fundamentally threatening to autonomous, controlled, rational, masculine corporeality (1994, 203). All of this thinking relies on boundary breaking, of moving beyond the presumptively fixed borders of the self-contained, rational Cartesian self towards something altogether different. No longer discrete, self-contained, rationally-organized entities, the bodies of feminist theorists are porous. They leak. They seep. They expel. This is theory that reimagines social relations through touch, on porosity, on connection.

But the more recent work of thinkers like Astrida Neimanis (2012, 2013, 2017) and Karin Amimoto Ingersoll (2016) moves beyond the fluxes and flows of the human body. The fluid is not just about the human, they argue. We need to situate ourselves—both our "watery bodies" (Neimanis 2012, 2013) and our knowledges—within a larger, more-than-human world. Imagining ourselves as watery bodies forces us to locate ourselves within rather than against the nonhuman world, and simultaneously, to acknowledge all watery bodies as having agency (Neimanis 2013, 27). This encounter between human and more-than-human paves the way for thinking through "hydro-logics"; that is, the ways in which water organizes itself. Water, Neimanis writes, can be simultaneously imagined as conduit, memory, archive, facilitator, and gestational milieu. It is past and present. It is intimate and planetary. What are the implications of all of this? Who are we, watered (Neimanis 2013)?

The inter-relatedness of human and the natural world is, of course, nothing new to Indigenous ways of knowing, which have stressed the larger ecologies of life, situating self within a thought world that is not premised on 'man's dominion over nature,' but rather on a symbiotic space where everything is interwoven; where the idea of 'life' includes all living things. Water, in such imaginings, is not passive or inert; rather, like Morrison's remembering river, this water is sentient, alive with its own intentionality (Anderson et al. 2013; Million 2014; Rose 2007). And yet water is also haunted, polluted with the violence of colonial histories (Alexander 2006; Probyn 2016; Walcott 2007). Indeed, as Patricia Nguyễn, who considers the memories of Vietnamese refugees, reminds us, water is "geopolitical material" (2017, 104). How do we manage these contradictions? Does water have memory? Does it leave bits and pieces of its DNA behind? What stories might a river tell and how might we be changed if we listen to them?

[SB]

REFERENCES

Alexander, M. Jacqui. 2006. *Pedagogies of crossing: Meditations on feminism, sexual politics, memory, and the sacred.* Durham: Duke University Press.
Anderson, Kim, Barbara Clow, and Margaret Haworth-Brockman. 2013. Carriers of water: Aboriginal women's experiences, relationships, and reflections. *Journal of Cleaner Production* 60: 11–17. https://doi.org/10.1016/j.jclepro.2011.10.023.
Bartlett, Alison. 2005. *Breastwork: Rethinking breastfeeding.* Sydney: University of New South Wales Press.
Cixous, Hélène. 1976. The laugh of the medusa. *Signs: Journal of Women in Culture and Society* 1 (4): 875–893.

Eades, Quinn. 2015. *All the beginnings: A queer autobiography of the body.* North Melbourne: Tantanoola.
Fisk, Harold. 1944. *Geological investigation of the alluvial valley of the lower Mississippi River.* Vicksburg: War Department Corps of Engineers.
Giles, Fiona. 2002. Fountains of love and loveliness: In praise of the dripping wet breast. *Journal of the Association for Research on Mothering* 4 (1): 7–18.
———. 2004. 'Relational and strange': A preliminary foray into a project to queer breastfeeding. *Australian Feminist Studies* 19 (45): 301–314. https://doi.org/10.1080/0816464042000278981.
———. 2005. The well-tempered breast: Fostering fluidity in breastly meaning and function. *Women's Studies* 34 (3–4): 301–326. https://doi.org/10.1080/00497870590964200.
Grosz, Elizabeth. 1994. *Volatile bodies: Towards a corporeal feminism.* Bloomington: Indiana University Press.
Ingersoll, Karin Amimoto. 2016. *Waves of knowing: A seascape epistemology.* Durham: Duke University Press.

Kristeva, Julia. 1982. *Powers of horror: An essay on abjection*. New York: Columbia University Press.

Longhurst, Robyn. 2001. *Bodies: Exploring fluid boundaries*. New York: Routledge.

———. 2008. *Maternities: Genders, bodies and space*. New York: Routledge.

Million, Dian. 2014. There is a river in me: Theory from life. In *Theorizing native studies*, ed. Audra Simpson and Andrea Smith, 31–42. Durham: Duke University Press.

Morrison, Toni. 1995. The site of memory. In *Inventing the truth: The art and craft of memoir*, ed. William Zinsser, 83–102. Boston and New York: Houghton Mifflin.

Neimanis, Astrida. 2012. Hydrofeminism: Or, on becoming a body of water. In *Undutiful daughters: New directions in feminist thought and practice*, ed. H. Gunkel, C. Nigianni, and F. Soderback, 96–115. New York: Palgrave Macmillan.

———. 2013. Feminist subjectivity, watered. *Feminist Review* 103: 23–31.

———. 2017. *Bodies of water: Posthuman feminist phenomenology*. Sydney: Bloomsbury.

Nguyễn, Patricia. 2017. Salt|water: Vietnamese refugee passages, memory, and statelessness at sea. *WSQ: Women's Studies Quarterly* 45 (1–2): 94–111. https://doi.org/10.1353/wsq.2017.0030.

Probyn, Elspeth. 2016. *Eating the ocean*. Durham: Duke University Press.

Rose, Deborah Bird. 2007. Justice and longing. In *Fresh water: New perspectives on water in Australia*, ed. Emily Potter, Alison Mackinnon, Stephen McKenzie, and Jennifer McKay, 8–20. Melbourne: Melbourne University Press.

Shaw, Rhonda, and Alison Bartlett, eds. 2010. *Giving breastmilk: Body ethics and contemporary breastfeeding practice*. Toronto: Demeter Press.

Shildrick, Margrit. 1997. *Leaky bodies and boundaries: Feminism, postmodernism, and (bio)ethics*. London and New York: Routledge.

Walcott, Derek. 2007. *Selected poems*. London: Farrar, Straus & Giroux.

Young, Iris Marion. 2005. *On female body experience: 'Throwing like a girl' and other essays*. New York and Toronto: Oxford University Press.

CHAPTER 9

Weather: Fog Trouble

Abstract Drawing on foggy experiences in St. John's, the capital and easternmost city of Newfoundland, this chapter considers fog as a sensorial bridge between the human and the more-than-human. While fog has often been imagined by Newfoundland writers as a force of erasure, disorientation, and loss, it might more productively be imagined otherwise. The closeness of fog does not obscure, as some have argued, but rather enables and heightens our remaining senses: sound, touch, smell, and taste. Its thick and heavy presence shows us new ways of engaging with the world.

Keywords Fog • Sense • Sensation • Intimacy • Erasure • Weather

Late one night in early December, I ventured out for a walk in the frozen fog around downtown St. John's. Squinting through the greyness all around me, breathing in moisture and feeling it on my skin, my body fastened itself to the heavy and moist air—my senses came alive. With deep nostril breathing came the scent of yeast rolling over the west side from the Labatt Brewery, whiffs of cigarette smoke and fast food lingering on Water Street, and traces of oil, wood varnish, and other abjections at the wharf in Harbourside Park.

On previous nights, I had heard the mournful call of foghorns. Who was out on the water? Would they find their way back home? Standing at the edge of the wharf, hearing waves fumble against each other in lops, I

© The Author(s) 2018
S. Boon et al., *Autoethnography and Feminist Theory at the Water's Edge*, https://doi.org/10.1007/978-3-319-90829-8_9

gazed at the ballast bed near me, drawn into the smooth, aging wood of the wharf and the stories I imagined it might reveal. Peering out into The Narrows, I wondered to what and to whom the wharf had borne witness. What beings and boats had pushed in through the greyness? I wanted to know fog stories. If it knew I was listening, how would it communicate? What would I learn?

The evocation of Newfoundland as place evokes a habitual closeness to fog. Sunny days in the capital city of St. John's, colloquially known as "Fogtown," are treasured. For decades, Newfoundlanders have written about and from the fog that many of us come to know as both an environmental companion and trouble. This amalgam of work illustrates sensuous connections between the environmental and the personal (Rodaway 1994). From foggy memory-writing of bodies in the Newfoundland landscape (Butler 1977), to imaginations of fog as a living thing (Murphy 1983), the lives of Newfoundlanders are caught up in foggy geographies.

Some islanders have highlighted the imperilling effects and beclouded affects of fog in the lives of those at the water's edge (Atkinson 1978; Pittman 1983). For Newfoundland fisherfolk in particular, fog at sea is something to be feared; it is unforgiving and snatches loved ones away (Pittman 1983). Because our livelihoods are historically and intimately connected to navigating the ocean, fog is sensuous and cartographic trouble. Yet, since we cannot control or manipulate it, how do we stay with the trouble (Haraway 2016) and stay in the fog? How and what can we learn from it?

On this island, fog has long been depicted as a spectral force of erasure, disorientation, and loss (Butts 2010). I want to argue for a new representation: I suggest that fog acts as a sensorial bridge between humans and other environmental bodies. While Newfoundland writing might be able to communicate the fearsomeness of fog, it can never describe fully the immersive experiences we undergo with the greyness. Islanders and fog share in a critical transcorporeal intimacy (Alaimo 2010; Neimanis and Loewen Walker 2014; Spivak 1999, 425; see also Chap. 5, earlier in this volume).

Surrounded by fog, islanders might at times lose our familiar senses of time and place, but its thick and heavy presence shows us new ways of engaging with the world. Within the fog, we become-with (Wright 2014), we theorize closeness (Bettcher and Goulimari 2017) with the environment (see also Chap. 7). We touch, smell, taste, hear, and feel our positionalities-in-place.

One August morning, thick and heavy with wet fog, I went hiking through forest trails in the east end of St. John's. I had consciously chosen to get lost in the greyness; I wanted to experiment with it. Most of all, I wanted to be alone with my thoughts. I wasn't aware that I would become-multiple with fog among the clouded woods. I didn't know the trails beforehand, and could only see a few feet in front of me at a time, so I made my own path through trees. The scent of damp earth, mud, wood, and moss lingered in the air and penetrated my body; the humidity moved through me with deep breaths, and moisture rested upon the surface of my skin. I was lifted through an aging forest. The fog told me stories, and drew me into an encounter with woody histories and lives. In this shrouded and intimate spacetime, I became foggy.

Astrida Neimanis and Rachel Loewen Walker imagine human and environmental bodies worlding together in a transcorporeal process of weathering (2014, 560). While Newfoundland writer Lisa Moore questions "how we belong to the landscape, yet are apart from it" (qtd. in O'Leary 2007, viii), I want to follow Neimanis and Loewen Walker to consider the ways that Newfoundlanders both form and are formed by fog, how we lift each other into being through the intimate proximities of advection. Earlier in this volume, I argued for a wet reconceptualization of sea ice in the lives of islanders (see Chap. 6). With those ideas still in mind, I wonder, too, if fog can offer insight into another kind of watered subjectivity (Neimanis 2013), or a form of "touching and feeling exceeding the corporeal" (Thien 2005, 192), that is caught up in the sensuous, foggy geographies Newfoundlanders call home.

[DJ]

References

Alaimo, Stacy. 2010. *Bodily natures: Science, environment, and the material self.* Bloomington: Indiana University Press.

Atkinson, Geoffrey. 1978. *Fog and its affects [sic] on the fishery in Newfoundland.* Unpublished manuscript, Centre for Newfoundland Studies.

Bettcher, Talia, and Pelagia Goulimari. 2017. Theorizing closeness: *A trans feminist conversation. Angelaki: Journal of the Theoretical Humanities* 22 (1): 49–60. https://doi.org/10.1080/0969725X.2017.1285608.

Butler, Gillian. 1977. Silver. In *From this place: A selection of writing by women of Newfoundland and Labrador*, ed. Bernice Morgan, Helen Porter, and Geraldine Rubia, 102. St. John's: Jesperson Printing Ltd.

Butts, Edward. 2010. *Ghost stories of Newfoundland and Labrador.* Toronto: Dundurn.

Haraway, Donna. 2016. *Staying with the trouble: Making kin in the chthulucene.* Durham: Duke University Press.

Murphy, Moya. 1983. Fog song. In *Stages: Literature of Newfoundland and Labrador book 2,* ed. Eric Norman, June Warr, and Ray Goulding, 118–119. St. John's: Breakwater Books.

Neimanis, Astrida. 2013. Feminist subjectivity, watered. *Feminist Review* 103: 23–41. https://doi.org/10.1057/fr.2012.25.

Neimanis, Astrida, and Rachel Loewen Walker. 2014. Weathering: Climate change and the 'thick time' of transcorporeality. *Hypatia* 29 (3): 558–575. https://doi.org/10.1111/hypa.12064.

O'Leary, Sheilagh. 2007. *Human natured: Newfoundland nudes.* Portugal Cove-St. Philip's: Boulder Publications.

Pittman, Al. 1983. In the black of night. In *Stages: Literature of Newfoundland and Labrador book 2,* ed. Eric Norman, June Warr, and Ray Goulding, 121–122. St. John's: Breakwater Books.

Rodaway, Paul. 1994. *Sensuous geographies: Body, sense, and place.* London and New York: Blackwell.

Spivak, Gayatri Chakravorty. 1999. *A critique of postcolonial reason: Toward a history of the vanishing present.* Cambridge: Harvard University Press.

Thien, Deborah. 2005. Intimate distances: Considering questions of 'us'. In *Emotional geographies,* ed. Joyce Davidson, Liz Bondi, and Mick Smith, 191–204. Aldershot: Ashgate.

Wright, Kate. 2014. Becoming-with: Living lexicon for the environmental humanities. *Environmental Humanities* 5: 277–281. https://doi.org/10.1215/22011919-3615514.

CHAPTER 10

Erosion: Fugitivity

Abstract This chapter builds links between the geographic phenomenon of erosion and Black and Indigenous engagements with fugitivity. In particular, it interrogates the possibilities of a fugitive geography, considering the idea of erosion not as destructive, but rather as revelatory. Noisy, exuberant, and excessive, a fugitive geography challenges notions of land and bodies controllable, countable, and containable. This chapter suggests that a fugitive approach to geography, as an opening to chaos, is an invitation to new ways of seeing.

Keywords Geography • Erosion • Fugitivity • Marronage

Summer snapshots, 2012. My older son, a mountain goat, scrabbling his way up the cliff face at Middle Cove Beach, a small cove just outside of St. John's, a cascade of tiny stones falling with his every step. He grasps at ledges, placing his feet carefully along ridges in the slate, concentration intense. All he ever wants is to go higher, to mold his body with rock. Far below, we stand at the shore, listening to the beach stones tumbling against one another. Middle Cove Beach reshapes itself with every storm, the pebbled landscape of hills and valleys moving with wind and water. One winter, the stones disappeared completely, leaving a sandy shore. But soon enough, they were back, their contours shaped by the waves. Above us, the cliff's craggy slate face changes, too, carved by ice storms and

© The Author(s) 2018   69
S. Boon et al., *Autoethnography and Feminist Theory at the Water's Edge*, https://doi.org/10.1007/978-3-319-90829-8_10

wind, but also by the endless, relentless climbing of children. Middle Cove Beach is at once timeless and ever-changing, static and mobile, solid and fluid.

Erosion suggests that geography is never mute, never passive; rather, through the interplay of weather, water, and land, it is continually asserting and creating itself, shifting, moving, shaping, and reshaping what otherwise appears to be solid, fixed, firm, certain. Just as bodily scars mark human journeys through life, so too does erosion scar land and seascapes, inscribing its histories into the flesh of the earth itself. The earth is haunted, its skin a living memory (Prosser 2001; Savage 2012).

Dictionary definitions suggest that to erode is to "gnaw away" ("erode, v." 2017); erosion is about being consumed, eaten up. In this sense, it is about insatiable desire. But erosion is also to "wear away, to eat out, to form a channel" ("erode, v." 2017); it is about hollowing, and in this way, about wounding and about revelation. As Hélène Cixous has observed, the wound is not just a site of horror; it is a site of germination (1998, xiv). What happens when we revel in the wound? Where might a reconsideration of erosion take us?

I want to think here about erosion as a process of fugitive geography, a disorderly geography that is chaotic, noisy, and fundamentally resistant to mapping. Within Black thought, fugitivity is linked with flight, a form of marronage, the flight of the enslaved from the plantation into the wild (Roberts 2015). But Black and Indigenous thinkers remind us that flight must also be understood at a metaphorical level (Campt 2017; Gumbs 2016; Martineau and Ritskes 2014; Ritskes 2017; Sharpe 2016; Simpson 2017; Sojoyner 2017). As a flight from oppressive power structures that have dictated the parameters of Black and Indigenous lives, fugitivity can be seen as an articulation of the fundamental impossibility of using "the master's tools" (Lorde 1984). But fugitivity is more than this; it is a refusal to pick up those tools in the first place (Gaztambide-Fernández 2014). This fugitive refusal, which gnaws away at the terms of imperialist and colonial domination, is inevitably wild, unruly, excessive, chaotic, dissonant, and anarchic (Gumbs 2016; Halberstam 2013; Harney and Moten 2013). It is improvisation in the face of fixity, disruption in the face of order, excess in the face of control.

How might we take erosion seriously within feminist thought? What are the possibilities of a fugitive geography of erosion that wears itself away, or of a mapped world in flight, fleeing from the frameworks that have been constructed to control it (Carter 2008)? And what might this world teach us about resistance, refusal, resurgence (Simpson 2017)?

Erosion happens when wind, land, sea, and living beings meet. Here in Newfoundland, that encounter is most often noisy and raucous. Ours is not a gentle ocean; it's a powerful, raging force whose imprint is felt not only in the jagged edges of our cliffs but in the countless memorials to fisherfolk lost at sea. Our ocean roars. It rushes. The encounter between salt, wind, water, and land is visceral, haunting both human memories and the gnawed-out coves where those memories live. Mapping this place must have been an imaginative adventure: how to mark land, claim it, possess it, conquer it, when that land appears to be made of solid rock? But simultaneously, how to make sense of the endless erosion of a jagged coastline?

If mapping is one of the tools of imperialist control, then what happens if the land itself refuses such imperatives? Fugitivity as a politics of refusal (Campt 2017, 96; see also Simpson 2017; Sojoyner 2017) is an invitation towards a new way of seeing, being, thinking (Campt 2017; Halberstam 2013; Ritskes 2017; Simpson 2017). Erosion—that encounter between wind, water, and land—enables a reading of a fugitive, fluid and ever-shifting geography of movement, a geography with its own meanings and its own intentionality (Bennett 2010; Tuana 2008). Erosion, and the silt, mud, and rocks that result, challenges the idea of land as property; as fixed, solid, controllable, containable. A rebellious, mobile, fluid, moving, shifting, and dissolving geography can also challenge notions of the controllable, countable, colonized body, whose being is subject to both physical and textual dismemberment, and whose value lies only in numbers—age, reproductive fecundity, worth (Hartman 2008; Philip 1989, 1997, 2008; Savage 2012; Simpson 2017, 14–5; see also Chap. 18, later in this volume).

Further, erosion is not just about gnawing desire; it is also about the debris that is left behind, the scraps of rocks, branches, trees, bodies, bones, and memories (Million 2014, 33; see also Lee 2016). Debris has traditionally been understood as mess, detritus, garbage. It is what we clean up after a storm, what we throw away after an earthquake. Debris is what we categorize as unsalvageable, unworthy, impure. It is danger, disease, threat. But Erica Violet Lee (2016), who theorizes the "wastelands," challenges us to imagine the apparently unworthy and unsalvageable differently. Proposing an ethics of gentleness and care, she writes, "the heart of wastelands theory is simple. Here, we understand that there is nothing and no one beyond healing" (2016, n.p.). What other stories might we find in debris; what other stories might reside in those scraps, fragments, and shards? Can we think of erosion as the wild (Harney and Moten 2013), as fugitive noise, exuberance, excess? What happens when we imagine it not as destructive but as revelatory?

As my son climbs and as the ocean roars, the winds howl, and the beach stones tumble, Middle Cove crumbles, shifts, stretches, and erodes, remaking itself in every encounter. Erosion offers a way of considering fugitivity—the fugitivity of Black and Indigenous thought, but also the fugitivity of geography itself. Fugitivity, here, might be understood as a site of entanglement (Barad 2007) where flight as refusal—enacted through the unruly, noisy, destructive, gnawing chaos of water, wind, and land—marks the terms of an inevitably haunted encounter.

[SB]

REFERENCES

Barad, Karen. 2007. *Meeting the universe halfway: Quantum physics and the entanglement of matter and meaning.* Durham: Duke University Press.
Bennett, Jane. 2010. *Vibrant matter: A political ecology of things.* Durham: Duke University Press.
Campt, Tina. 2017. *Listening to images.* Durham: Duke University Press.
Carter, Paul. 2008. *Dark writing: Geography, performance, design.* Honolulu: University of Hawaii Press.
Cixous, Hélène. 1998. *Stigmata: Escaping texts.* London and New York: Routledge.
"erode, v." *OED Online.* 2017, June. Oxford University Press. http://www.oed.com.qe2a-proxy.mun.ca/view/Entry/64061?redirectedFrom=erode. Accessed 3 Jan 2018.
Gaztambide-Fernández, Rubén. 2014. Decolonial options and artistic/aesthesic entanglements: An interview with Walter Mignolo. *Decolonization: Indigeneity, Education & Society* 3 (1): 196–212.
Gumbs, Alexis Pauline. 2016. *Spill: Scenes of black feminist fugitivity.* Durham: Duke University Press.
Halberstam, Jack. 2013. Go gaga: Anarchy, chaos, and the wild. *Social Text 116* 31 (3): 123–134. https://doi.org/10.1215/01642472-2152873.
Harney, Stefano, and Fred Moten. 2013. *The undercommons: Fugitive planning and black study.* New York: Autonomedia.
Hartman, Saidiya. 2008. Venus in two acts. *Small Axe: A Caribbean Journal of Criticism* 26: 1–14. https://doi.org/10.2979/SAX.2008.-.26.1.

Lee, Erica Violet. 2016. In defence of the wastelands: A survival guide. *GUTS 7.* http://gutsmagazine.ca/wastelands/. Accessed 31 Dec 2017.

Lorde, Audre. 1984. *Sister outsider: Essays and speeches.* Trumansburg, NY: Crossing Press Feminist Series.

Martineau, Jarrett, and Eric Ritskes. 2014. Fugitive indigeneity: Reclaiming the terrain of decolonial struggle through Indigenous art. *Decolonization: Indigeneity, Education & Society* 3 (1): i–xiii.

Million, Dian. 2014. There is a river in me: Theory from life. In *Theorizing native studies*, ed. Audra Simpson and Andrea Smith, 31–42. Durham: Duke University Press.

Philip, M. NourbeSe. 1989. Discourse on the logic of language. In *She tries her tongue/her silence softly breaks*, 56–59. Charlottetown: Ragweed Press.

———. 1997. Dis/Place. In *A genealogy of resistance—And other essays*, 74–112. Toronto: The Mercury Press.

———. 2008. *Zong!* Middletown: Wesleyan University Press.

Prosser, Jay. 2001. Skin memories. In *Thinking through the skin*, ed. Sara Ahmed and Jackie Stacey, 52–68. London and New York: Routledge.

Ritskes, Eric. 2017. Beyond and against white settler capitalism in Palestine: Fugitive futurities in Amir Nizar Zuabi's "The underground ghetto city of Gaza". *Cultural Studies ↔ Critical Methodologies* 17 (1): 78–86. https://doi. org/10.1177/1532708616640561.

Roberts, Neil. 2015. *Freedom as marronage*. Chicago: University of Chicago Press.

Savage, Candace. 2012. *A geography of blood: Unearthing memory from a prairie landscape*. Vancouver: Greystone Books.

Sharpe, Christina. 2016. *In the wake: On Blackness and being*. Durham: Duke University Press.

Simpson, Leanne Betasamosake. 2017. *As we have always done: Indigenous freedom through radical resistance*. Minneapolis and London: University of Minnesota Press.

Sojoyner, Damien M. 2017. Another life is possible: Fugitivity and enclosed spaces. *Cultural Anthropology* 32 (4): 514–536. https://doi.org/10.14506/ca32.4.04.

Tuana, Nancy. 2008. Viscous porosity: Witnessing Katrina. In *Material feminisms*, ed. Stacy Alaimo and Susan Hekman, 188–213. Bloomington and Indianapolis: Indiana University Press.

CHAPTER 11

Place: Re/mapping

Abstract This chapter seeks to "re-map" the conventional processes and practices of cartography. Drawing in particular on the work of Indigenous and Black writers and thinkers, among them Mishuana Goeman, Katherine McKittrick, and Dionne Brand, as well as on the work of Fred Wah and Gloria Anzaldúa, this chapter focuses primarily on conceptual and imaginative geographies, looking at questions of memory, metaphor, myths, and origins as ways of re-mapping identity and belonging.

Keywords Maps • Place • Placelessness • Memory • Belonging

Growing up with a geographer as a mother meant that there were always maps, globes, and atlases around the house. They allowed me to appreciate the incredible vastness of the world but simultaneously made me aware of boundaries: the physical boundaries of water and land, as well as the political boundaries of nations and states. I can recall flipping through an atlas on our coffee table as a child, fascinated by the difference between various geographical perspectives. I would look at the gradations and colours of the physical maps—representing mountains, rivers, and other geographic formations—and then compare them to the more geometric, flat appearance of the political maps. How different these perspectives were, and yet somehow, impossibly, they each represented the 'same' world. In a way, the variations between maps revealed to me that there was

© The Author(s) 2018
S. Boon et al., *Autoethnography and Feminist Theory at the Water's Edge*, https://doi.org/10.1007/978-3-319-90829-8_11

no *true* representation of the places in which we lived. Geological time, geographical shifts, and political contestations, all called for a reimagining of lines: of borders, states, countries, and landscapes.

If anything, the changes in our maps prove the fallibility of traditional cartography, and the fictions of place (Brand 2001, 18; see also Kelly 2009, and Chap. 17, later in this volume). To navigate those intricate boundaries, we might ask ourselves: What are the implications of these lines on a map? Where do we carve the borders of belonging (see also Chaps. 10 and 20)? How do we chart the journey of one's self? Can stories effectively map our world(s)? While maps may well represent the worlds in which we live, countless other stories exist both beyond—and because of—the cartographer's lines.

In *Mark my words: Native women mapping our nations*, Mishuana Goeman describes maps as powerful tools that have been historically central to colonial rule (2013, 16). She suggests that the power of mapping has become normalized by the common perception that it is simply objective, when in reality it has been a means to control, metaphorically and physically, both land and bodies (2013, 16; see also Bushell 2012; Del Casino and Hanna 2000; Harley 1988; Mills 2005; Radcliffe 2011; Tsing 2012). In an attempt to disrupt the dominance of traditional mapping techniques, Goeman asks, "What happens when the poet takes over the cartographer's tools?" (2013, 119). Through close analyses of Native women's poetry and prose, Goeman shows how creative writing helps reveal the continued influence of settler colonialism on contemporary identities, and how these writers work to (re)map colonial geographies and cartographies. By approaching Native women's writing as "non-normative geographies," Goeman highlights how issues of space, place, identity, and belonging are often rooted in heteropatriarchal histories of colonialism, slavery, and orientalism (2013, 4–22). As an alternative geography, writing becomes a powerful and poetic tool with which to map our world, our land, and our selves.

While Goeman focuses on Indigenous experiences of, and resistance to, traditional mapping, there are parallels between her arguments and those of other "categorized, colonized, and subjugated" groups (2013, 119). Goeman's poetic cartography is reminiscent of Black feminist geographic perspectives. For example, a "poetics of landscape," a term originating from Édouard Glissant and explored further by Katherine McKittrick, acknowledges the significance of "geographic expression" through "saying, theorizing, feeling, knowing, writing, and imagining space and place"

(McKittrick 2006, xxii). This approach stretches the cartographic compass further, opening up the space of the body as a reimagined site of geographic inquiry (Blake 1793; Philip 1997; see also Chap. 7, earlier in this volume). A poetics of landscape thus acts as a "counterconcept" to conventional geographies (Wynter 1989, 639; see also McKittrick 2006, xxii), resisting their seemingly unquestionable authority and "deceptively simple" ways of relating to the land (Goeman 2013, 16). Just as Goeman understands Native women's poetry as a powerful method of decolonization, Glissant's poetics of landscape allow Black women in particular to reclaim, rename, and reimagine the relationship between land, history, and self.

(Re)mapping can take us beyond the material landscape, drawing instead on the power of memory and imagination. In *A map to the Door of No Return*, Dionne Brand is skeptical of how traditional geographic and cartographic epistemologies can effectively chart her particular experiences of placelessness as a Black woman (Brand 2001, 24–9; see also McKittrick 2006, 104–5). The concept of the Door of No Return is crucial to this theoretical, geographic conflict. While Brand admits that cartographers have charted maps to the Door of No Return over many years, these physical renderings merely depict the door's cartographic materiality (2001, 2). The Door of No Return exists not through its coordinates, but rather, through the minds of those living in the Diaspora; it is not only physical, but spiritual in its existence (Brand 2001, 2, 18–21). Brand imagines her enslaved ancestors stepping through this door towards slave ships and finds herself, through reflection, also caught in this impossibly real space *between* the door—the inherited, inhabited, "inexplicable space" of the Diaspora (Brand 2001, 20). Simultaneously tangible and intangible, the Door of No Return represents the connections between past and present, and the contradictions between longing and belonging within the spaces—both physical and fictional—of the Black Diaspora. The door is not just one place on a map, but instead a "collection of places" (Brand 2001, 18) metaphoric, mythical, and un/mappable. How can the cartographer's tools account for a place that is simultaneously real and imagined, a place both absent and present (Brand 2001, 19, 21; see also Chap. 12, later in this volume)? How might they account for a place that is multiple? Can they map the myths? Can they chart one's consciousness?

Like Brand, Fred Wah (2006) navigates experiences of race, identity, and belonging in Canada through a mapping metaphor. Early in *Diamond grill*, a poetic "biotext" (Wah 2006, 184) that reflects on his experiences with hybridity and multiculturalism as a hyphenated Chinese-Canadian,

Wah writes, "[m]aps don't have beginnings, just edges" (2006, 1). This idea not only hints at the theoretical gaps in the practice and process of mapping, but also alludes to Wah's writing style as theory in itself. Like Brand, Wah conceptualizes writing as a mapping of self. Not *the* map of *the* self, but *a* map of *a* self (Wah 2006, 185). In the afterword that follows the main text, Wah writes, "I don't want the narrative to feel too settled and defined or concluded, so, as is characteristic of the long poem, the resistance to closure becomes, in a sense, a resistance to plot and story" (2006, 181). In a way, Wah uses poetic writing to resist being plotted within traditional literary styles, in much the same way as he resists being charted—mapped—by his cultural origins.

Instead, using the imagery of a swinging door between the kitchen of his family's Chinese restaurant and the adjoining dining room filled with white settler Canadians, a recurring motif in the book, Wah projects a sense of inbetweenness—a hyphen—through the spatial dynamics of the setting and the characters (2006, 176). The hinges of the door, like the hyphen between "Chinese" and "Canadian," represent the disjunction between multiculturalism and belonging (Wah 2006, 178–9). Journeying back and forth between the hyphenated door, Wah creates a sense of being culturally un/mappable. Like the Door of No Return, Wah's hyphenated door represents a sense of placelessness, of inbetweenness. As the door has no discernible beginning or ending, origins become both blurred and arbitrary (Brand 2001, 64; see also Cixous and Calle-Gruber 1997 and Chap. 4, earlier in this volume).

This is not to suggest that origins are unimportant. But a closer look at myths of origin may be in order (Brand 2001, 85). Canada, in particular, has constructed the idea of origin based on the arbitrary pursuit of "degrees of belonging" (Brand 2001, 64; see also Bannerji 2000). In other words, belonging requires one to fit neatly into a narrative, one that assumes a clear, mappable origin story. Indeed, like Wah, Brand finds that it is this expectation to *be* longing for origins that actually fuels the artificiality of belonging. Writing one's own narrative thus works to unsettle the "master narrative" of Canadian citizenship and the illusions of progressive multiculturalism (Fleischmann and Van Styvendale 2011, xx).

Borders, the work of Brand and Wah suggests, are in flux; they may be porous, and they have a significant impact on both personal and collective experiences of identity (Wicks 2010, 140). Gloria Anzaldúa (2012) similarly conceives of borders through the tensions between identity and place. Here, borders represent not only physical crossings, but also cultural, racial, and ideological crossings (Anzaldúa 2012, 99). For Anzaldúa, a world defined by borders and boundaries cannot account for her *mestiza* consciousness (2012, 99). It is only when we embrace the ambiguity of identities—beyond the borders and walls of the dominant, white patriarchal culture—that we can work towards a be/longing that "includes rather than excludes" (Anzaldúa 2012, 100–1). As Daze Jefferies (see Chap. 2) points out, it is particularly necessary as a white settler Canadian to critically consider 'our' own poetics of landscape and sense of belonging alongside colonial disruptions of space and place. After all, the borders within which 'we' reside—physically and metaphorically—represent the continued hauntings of colonial histories (Goeman 2013; Tuck and Ree 2013).

In a nation founded on the exclusionary practices of colonial conquest, belonging seems to be merely an illusion. However, if we take Goeman's lead and search for alternative approaches to (re)mapping, maybe we can begin to see belonging (and its longings) as something beyond the nationalism-cloaked-in-multiculturalism outlook that Canada seems to prescribe. If we displace the traditional origin story and instead look to non-normative geographies, like Brand's Door of No Return, or Wah's hyphenated kitchen door, perhaps we can learn something about the complexities of belonging that are not necessarily easy to map out. After all, "power inheres in our stories" (Goeman 2013, 3; see also King 2003)—from beginnings and endings, to the endless space beyond the edges.

[LB]

References

Anzaldúa, Gloria. 2012. *Borderlands/La frontera: The new mestiza.* 4th ed. San Francisco: Aunt Lute Books.
Bannerji, Himani. 2000. *The dark side of the nation: Essays on multiculturalism, nationalism, and gender.* Toronto: Canadian Scholars Press.
Blake, William. 1793. *Visions of the daughters of Albion.* London: Blake.
Brand, Dionne. 2001. *A map to the Door of No Return.* Toronto: Vintage Canada.
Bushell, Sally. 2012. The slipperiness of literary maps: Critical cartography and literary cartography. *Cartographica* 46 (3): 149–160. https://doi.org/10.3138/carto.47.3.1202.
Cixous, Hélène, and Mireille Calle-Gruber. 1997. *Hélène Cixous, Rootprints: Memory and life writing.* Trans. Eric Prenowitz. New York: Routledge.

Del Casino, Vincent J., Jr., and Stephen P. Hanna. 2000. Representations and identities in tourism map spaces. *Progress in Human Geography* 24 (1): 23–46. https://doi.org/10.1191/030913200673388638.

Fleischmann, Aloys N.M., and Nancy Van Styvendale. 2011. Introduction: Narratives of citizenship. In *Narratives of citizenship: Indigenous and diasporic peoples unsettle the nation-state*, ed. Aloys N.M. Fleischmann, Nancy Van Styvendale, and Cody McCarroll, xi–xlv. Edmonton: University of Alberta Press.

Goeman, Mishuana. 2013. *Mark my words: Native women mapping our nations.* Minneapolis: University of Minnesota Press.

Harley, J.B. 1988. Maps, knowledge and power. In *The iconography of landscape*, ed. D. Cosgrove and S. Daniels, 277–312. Cambridge: University of Cambridge Press.

Kelly, Ursula. 2009. *Migration and education in a multicultural world: Culture, loss, and identity.* New York: Palgrave Macmillan.

King, Thomas. 2003. *The truth about stories: A Native narrative.* Toronto: House of Anansi.

McKittrick, Katherine. 2006. *Demonic grounds: Black women and the cartographies of struggle.* Minneapolis: University of Minnesota Press.

Mills, Sara. 2005. *Gender and colonial space.* Manchester and New York: Manchester University Press.

Philip, M. NourbeSe. 1997. Dis/Place: The space between. In *A genealogy of resistance—And other essays*, 74–112. Toronto: Mercury Press.

Radcliffe, Sarah A. 2011. Third space, abstract space and coloniality: National and subaltern cartography in Ecuador. In *Postcolonial spaces: The politics of place in contemporary culture*, ed. Andrew Teverson and Sara Upstone, 129–145. Houndmills: Palgrave Macmillan.

Tsing, Anna. 2012. Unruly edges: Mushrooms as companion species. *Environmental Humanities* 1: 141–154. https://doi.org/10.1215/22011919-3610012.

Tuck, Eve, and C. Ree. 2013. A glossary of haunting. In *Handbook of autoethnography*, ed. Stacey Holman Jones, Tony E. Adams, and Carolyn Ellis, 639–658. Walnut Grove: Left Coast Press.

Wah, Fred. 2006. *Diamond grill.* Edmonton: NeWest Press.

Wicks, Jennifer. 2010. Navigating borders: Language and culture—Inside and outside. In *Despite this loss: Essays on culture, memory and identity in Newfoundland and Labrador*, ed. Ursula A. Kelly and Elizabeth Yeoman, 137–156. St. John's: ISER Books.

Wynter, Sylvia. 1989. Beyond the word of man: Glissant and the new discourse of the Antilles. *World Literature Today* 63 (4): 637–648. https://doi.org/10.2307/40145557.

PART III

Languages

CHAPTER 12

Colonialism: Ruins

Abstract This chapter considers the conceptual potential of ruin and ruination. Drawing on the work of Brian Dillon, Rebecca Solnit, Toni Morrison, Ann Laura Stoler, Audre Lorde, Eve Tuck and C. Ree, this chapter suggests that ruins are unsettling but also, a necessary step towards social change. Indeed, ruin's haunted, crumbling structures—material, metaphorical, and embodied—reveal the artifice of imperial and colonial processes and practices.

Keywords Ruin • Ruination • Unsettle • Haunting

When I was eighteen, I worked as a server at Coady's Eatery, a fish and chips restaurant in my hometown. As it had been for many others in my community, this was my first experience in the service industry. A small, locally-owned place characterized by its retro 'traditional-Newfoundland-fast-food-meets-1950s-ice-cream-parlour' atmosphere, Coady's served locals and tourists, both young and old. It had been a staple in our community for as long as I could remember, an integral part of the place I called home. And yet, a few years after I left my job, Coady's closed its doors without any explanation, its windows dimmed and filled with mystery. Today, though its sign is long gone, and its once vibrant green exterior is fading, the building still remains. While the community's fish and chips cravings have been satisfied by other enterprises, the presence of the abandoned building somehow accentuates the feeling of absence. With lights off, doors locked, and parking lot empty (save for the occasional snowplough), the site—and sight—remains a ruin upon the landscape. Subtle, but still spectral. Ruins of the past; a haunting presence.

What counts as a ruin? *When* does something become a ruin? Ruins are usually perceived as mysterious, desolate spaces (Stoler 2008, 194). Often, we imagine them as the crumbling structures of once grand civilizations, now abandoned, dusty, and covered in ivy (Stoler 2008, 194; Tuck and Ree 2013, 653). Ruins have thus come to represent loss and decay, or what has become absent from the past (Stoler 2008, 194). In this sense, they shape our sense of time, drawing attention to the enigmatic confluence of time and history (Dillon 2011, 11). As both "a remnant of, and portal into, the past," ruins serve as a perpetual reminder of the passing of time (Dillon 2011, 11). As "petrified life," ruins take our psyche from the past, the present, and towards possible futures (Benjamin, qtd. in Stoler 2008, 194; see also Dillon 2011, 11; Ferreday and Kuntsman 2011; Gordon 2011). And still, "ruination is a corrosive process that weighs on the future and shapes the present" (Stoler 2008, 194). "To ruin," which gestures toward disaster and destruction, is, as Ann Laura Stoler points out, a "vibrantly violent verb" (2008, 194). The corrosiveness of ruination points not only to imperial relics upon the landscape, but to the imperial effects upon lives and their histories (Stoler 2008, 194). Ruins represent not only historical nostalgia, but also alternative histories; contained in ruins are the "visible and visceral senses" through which colonialism remains (Stoler 2008, 194–6). What, then, can ruins teach us through this temporal and visceral journey?

On my island home of Newfoundland, ruins might conjure images of abandoned rural outport communities. In a twenty-year period between 1954 and 1975, some 300 communities across the island were resettled for the purposes of economic and political progress (Manning 2017, 10; see also Blake 2015). While some families used boats to move their houses across water to larger communities, others had to leave their homes behind and start anew. Despite the progressive aims of resettlement, ruins and ruination—both material and metaphorical—were an unfortunate reality for many (Mayda 2004; "The resettlement program" 2006; for an alternative reading, see Blake 2015).

Going further back in time, one might also envision the ruins of Viking settlers at the archaeological site of L'Anse aux Meadows, located on the northernmost tip of the main island of Newfoundland. Or perhaps we might turn to Port aux Choix, along the island's west coast, where archaeological ruins show how different Indigenous groups lived over time, long before European settlers arrived (Bell and Renouf 2005, 2). These histories are buried into our landscapes, leaving hints of stories behind.

But in what other ways do ruins unsettle our contemporary landscapes? What happens if we look beyond the romantic visions of ruins? For Eve Tuck and C. Ree, ruins exist most profoundly in the colonial legacy of contemporary buildings and cityscapes (2013, 653). Here, "the quick turnover of buildings, disappearing landmarks, and disposable homes" comes to represent an alternative, but equally accurate, image of ruins (Tuck and Ree 2013, 653). Buildings, landmarks, and homes are made and remade, even before they have the chance to crumble. These contemporary ruins become reintegrated into our everyday lives, representing "the living dead who endlessly haunt the landscape, preventing it from ever becoming peaceful again" (Picon 2000, 76–7). While colonialism is often concealed through displays of hegemonic domination, ruins, in a way, become a tangible representation of colonial ruination (Stoler 2008, 194).

So, too, might we consider absence as a form of ruination. A haunted cityscape, built and rebuilt out of ever-growing piles of rubble, carries within it the absent presence of those Indigenous peoples who once lived fully on Turtle Island. But space, itself, might also be understood to be haunted; even our most isolated places are never truly empty (Goldman 2012, 42; Haddour 2000, 103; see also Savage 2012). Seemingly empty land evokes the "haunting fear" of an unidentifiable presence; this presence through absence transforms unsettled landscapes from something awe-inspiring into something spectrally awful (Goldman 2012, 42). The ghosts of colonialism remind white settlers that they will never be truly alone, neither in the wilderness, nor in the city (Gordon 2011; Haddour 2000; Jarvis 1998, 68; Tuck and Ree 2013).

Ruins, these ghosts suggest, are never silent. Indeed, as Caws observes, "the ruins look back" (qtd. in Tuck and Ree 2013, 653); that is, ruins are a persistent haunting, a constant presence that speaks even through its silence. Ruins are not remnants of the past; rather, they are part and parcel of our everyday lives (Tuck and Ree 2013). Inside them, we can see, feel, and hear the threat of the past in the present. Ruins become both evidence and erasure—through history and destruction, and through experience and memory (Solnit 2011, 151). They are a constant becoming; resilient, restorative, affective (Solnit 2011, 151). Ruins keep us in suspension, prompting us to "unsettle our sense of place" (Tuck and Ree 2013, 653).

To unsettle is "to deprive of fixity or quiet" ("unsettle, v." 2018). We might think here of unsettled stomachs, unsettled sleep, unsettled minds. An unsettled body is a body shaped by its affective engagements with the world. What might ruination mean at the level of embodied experience? I am unsettled by histories of colonial violence and indigenous erasure. What of linguistic assimilation, where colonial hegemony manifests itself corporeally?

In Canada, residential schools were built and used to assimilate Indigenous children into white settler culture. Between the 1880s and 1990s, thousands of children were separated from their families, stripped of their names and cultural and spiritual traditions, and banned from speaking their native languages in favour of English or French (Hanson 2009; Truth and Reconciliation Commission of Canada 2012; Truth and Reconciliation Commission of Canada, Fontaine, and Craft 2016; Wolochatiuk 2012; see also Million 2009). These residential schools, as literal structures designed to impose the hegemonic aims of white settler nationalism, are also representations of the ideological structures of colonialism in action. While these schools have since closed, and reconciliation is in (troubled) process, the legacy of colonialism carries on through contemporary experiences (and absences) of language and culture (Million 2009; Wolochatiuk 2012). Colonial hegemony manifests itself corporeally. As M. NourbeSe Philip suggests, reflecting on the violence of transatlantic slavery, language becomes a bodily "l/anguish" (Philip 1989, 56). Here, the ruins of colonial structures—both in matter and in mind—tangle in the tongue. They leave lingering debris through the ruination not only of landscapes, but also of lives (Philip 1989, 56; Stoler 2008, 194; for another reading of debris see Chap. 10, earlier in this volume).

This is not to suggest, however, that ruination is not reparable. As Audre Lorde has famously claimed, "the masters tools will never dismantle the master's house" (1984, 112). For Lorde, ruin is a necessary step towards social change. To move towards restitution is to reject the tools that actively conserve the structures of colonialism and to find alternative tools with which to enter our haunted ruins. We must become aware of the "hauntedness of our own language" (Regenspan 2014, 119). This would entail, for example, acknowledging the hegemonic nature of the English language, of the lingering ruination within the words we use (Macedo et al. 2003; see also Brand 2001; Philip 1989). Later in this volume, I examine how silence can be repurposed as a tool against the colonial repression of language (see Chap. 14). How, then, might ruins serve as a model for exploring the oppressive structures of colonialism upon language?

In her "Nobel lecture in literature," Toni Morrison surveys the "systematic looting of language" throughout history (2008, 201). She considers the philosophical contours of language, drawing from the myth of the Tower of Babel. As the story goes, the tower, encumbered by the weight of multiple languages, collapsed before it could ascend to the heavens (Morrison 2008, 202). While it was said that one monolithic language would have strengthened the building, Morrison is skeptical of this necessarily narrow path towards a so-called heaven (Morrison 2008, 202). She notes that if they had "take[n] the time to understand other languages, other views, other narratives ... the heaven they imagined might have been found at their feet" (Morrison 2008, 202). As the tower falls, it pulls with it a veil from these imperial ideals. Here, the crumbling structures represent the potential of language, the possibility of resistance, and the power of ruins.

Like the haunted ruins of Canada's residential school system, the Tower of Babel collapses under the weight of history, and under the idealistic, illusory aims of a singular, 'superior' language. These colonial aims of building upward to an unattainable heaven, and transforming tongues along the way, are evident in not only the ruins found in myth, but in the ruins around us. Through these ruins, we see how the past permeates place, perpetually affects the present, and shapes the possibility of our futures (Gordon 2011; Jarvis 1998, 127; Stoler 2008, 194). We should remember, as Stoler points out, "ruins are not found, they are made" (2008, 201). How then, do we make ruins? What do we acknowledge as ruins? As ruins haunt and unsettle us, we must consider the affective process of ruins and ruination upon our contemporary lives. So too, must we address the histories that hauntings unsettle. Even through the ruinations of language, ruins speak to us through their stillness, their silence. Ruins have histories. Ruins tell stories. We may be looking, but are we learning?

[LB]

REFERENCES

Bell, Trevor, and M.A.P. Renouf. 2005. Introduction. *Newfoundland and Labrador Studies* 20 (1): 1–7.

Blake, Raymond B. 2015. The resettlement of Pushthrough, Newfoundland, in 1969. *Newfoundland and Labrador Studies* 30 (2): 220–245.

Brand, Dionne. 2001. *A map to the Door of No Return: Notes to belonging*. Toronto: Vintage Canada.

Dillon, Brian. 2011. Introduction. In *Ruins*, ed. Brian Dillon, 10–19. Cambridge: MIT Press; London: Whitechapel Gallery.

Ferreday, Debra, and Adi Kuntsman. 2011. Haunted futurities. *Borderlands E-Journal* 10 (2): no page.

Goldman, Marlene. 2012. *DisPossession: Haunting in Canadian fiction.* Ebook. Montreal: McGill-Queen's University Press.

Gordon, Avery. 2011. Some thoughts on haunting and futurity. *Borderlands E-Journal* 10 (2): no page.

Haddour, Azzedine. 2000. *Colonial myths: History and narrative.* Manchester: Manchester University Press.

Hanson, Erin. 2009. The residential school system. *First Nations and Indigenous studies: The University of British Columbia.* http://indigenousfoundations.arts. ubc.ca/the_residential_school_system/. Accessed 21 Feb 2018.

Jarvis, Brian. 1998. *Postmodern cartographies: The geographical imagination in contemporary American culture.* New York: St. Martin's Press.

Lorde, Audre. 1984. *Sister outsider: Essays and speeches.* Trumansburg, NY: Crossing Press Feminist Series.

Macedo, Donaldo, Bessie Dendrinos, and Panayota Gounari. 2003. *The hegemony of English.* Boulder: Paradigm Publishers.

Manning, Susan M. 2017. Contrasting colonisations: (Re)storying Newfoundland/ Ktaqmkuk as place. *Settler Colonial Studies.* Online First. https://doi.org/10. 1080/2201473X.2017.1327010.

Mayda, Chris. 2004. Resettlement in Newfoundland, again. *American Geographcal Society's Focus on Geography* 48 (1): 27–32. https://doi.org/10.1111/ j.1949-8535.2004.tb00133.x.

Million, Dian. 2009. Felt theory: An Indigenous feminist approach to affect and history. *Wicazo Sa Review* 24 (2): 53–76. https://doi.org/10.1353/ wic.0.0043.

Morrison, Toni. 2008. The Nobel lecture in literature. In *What moves at the margin: Selected nonfiction*, ed. Carolyn C. Denard, 198–207. Jackson: University Press of Mississippi.

Philip, M. NourbeSe. 1989. Discourse on the logic of language. In *She tries her tongue, her silence softly breaks*, 55–60. Charlottetown: Ragweed Press.

Picon, Antoine. 2000. Anxious landscapes: From the ruin to rust. Trans. Karen Bates. *Grey Room* 1: 64–83. https://doi.org/10.1162/152638100750173065.

Regenspan, Barbara. 2014. *Haunting and the educational imagination.* Rotterdam: Sense Publishers.

Savage, Candace. 2012. *A geography of blood: Unearthing memory from a prairie landscape.* Vancouver: Greystone Books.

Solnit, Rebecca. 2011. The ruins of memory. In *Ruins*, ed. Brian Dillon, 150–52. Cambridge: MIT Press; London: Whitechapel Gallery.

Stoler, Ann Laura. 2008. Imperial debris: Reflections on ruins and ruination. *Cultural Anthropology* 23 (2): 191–219. https://doi.org/10.1525/ can.2008.23.2.191.

The Resettlement Program. 2006. *The Newfoundland and Labrador heritage web site*. http://www.heritage.nf.ca/articles/politics/resettlement-program.php. Accessed 19 Feb 2018.

Truth and Reconciliation Commission of Canada. 2012. *Canada, Aboriginal peoples, and residential schools: They came for the children*. Winnipeg: Truth and Reconciliation Commission of Canada.

Truth and Reconciliation Commission of Canada, Phil Fontaine and Aimee Craft. 2016. *A knock on the door: The essential history of residential schools from the Truth and Reconciliation Commission of Canada*. Winnipeg: University of Manitoba Press.

Tuck, Eve, and C. Ree. 2013. A glossary of haunting. In *Handbook of autoethnography*, ed. Stacey Holman Jones, Tony E. Adams, and Carolyn Ellis, 639–658. Walnut Creek: Left Coast Press.

"unsettle, v." OED Online. 2018, January. Oxford University Press. http://www. oed.com.qe2a-proxy.mun.ca/view/Entry/217786?redirectedFrom=unsettle# eid. Accessed 20 Feb 2018.

Wolochatiuk, Tim. 2012. *We were children*. Montreal: National Film Board of Canada; Eagle Vision; Entertainment One.

CHAPTER 13

Histories: Stitching Theory

Abstract This chapter considers handcraft, an intimate, reflective—and reflexive—activity through which generations of women have made sense of their lives, as a site of theory making. Bringing together scholarship on knitting, cooking, quilting, and craftivism, it asserts that handcraft, as process-oriented work, is a form of both life writing and theory making through which we stitch ourselves and our thinking into being.

Keywords Handcraft • Stitching • Embodiment • Craftivism

When winter has its way with Newfoundland, blizzard conditions bring dramatic snowdrifts and muscles that ache from shoveling. Whole communities shut down: schools, government offices, the university, banks, public transit. Even the shopping mall and the liquor store close. And in that suspended space-time of howling wind, blowing snow, and surging tides, we—my family and I—cocoon ourselves inside, savouring hot chocolate and scones between bouts of shoveling. One blizzarding morning, as the snowdrifts rise, I find myself in front of the sewing machine, stitching a quilt together.

Embroidery, knitting, crocheting—all have experienced a resurgence in recent years. But what does this mean? What conceptual purposes might handcraft, traditionally aligned with the domestic and the feminine, serve? Handcraft has been, and continues to be, a way for women to claim

© The Author(s) 2018
S. Boon et al., *Autoethnography and Feminist Theory at the Water's Edge*, https://doi.org/10.1007/978-3-319-90829-8_13

citizenship, to give voice to the issues that concern them and their communities most, and to contribute to what might be deemed 'the greater good.' For Ricia Chansky, for example, craft work is simultaneously destructive and creative: "The needle stabs as it creates, forcing thread or yarn into the act of creation. From a violent action comes the birth of a new whole. Women are channeling their rage, frustration, guilt, and other difficult emotions into a powerfully productive activity" (2010, 682; see also Vaccaro 2010, 2015, and Chap. 16, later in this volume). Central to Chansky's analysis is a linkage between social justice, emotion, and generative action. I would argue that theory emerges at the exact point where these three elements meet; that is, in the process of creation itself.

A considerable body of research has considered the role of handcrafts—sewing, knitting, crocheting, and the like—in the service of activism. We might consider here Rozsika Parker's influential *The subversive stitch* (1984/2011), Gillian Elinor et al.'s *Women and craft* (1987), and more recently, Betsy Greer's publications, *Craftivism: The art of craft and activism* (2014), and *Knitting for good: A guide to creating personal, social, and political change, stitch by stitch* (2008), but also the ever-growing body of scholarly literature on contemporary craftivism and DIY culture (see, for example: Black 2017; Boon and Pentney 2017; Bratich and Brush 2011; Clarke 2016; Fields 2014; Groeneveld 2010; Kelly 2014; Luckman 2013; Pentney 2008; Springgay et al. 2011; Springgay 2010; Williams 2011).

Handcraft as a form of citizenship has a long history on this island I call home. During the First World War, women's knitting and sewing supported the efforts of the Women's Patriotic Association, as women across the island knitted thousands upon thousands of pairs of grey socks for the men of the Royal Newfoundland Regiment (Cullum 1995; Duley 1916; Warren 1998, 2005). Later, these same women marshaled their skills in service of the Newfoundland Outport Nursing and Industrial Association (NONIA), knitting and selling their wares to raise funds for nursing care in remote communities (House 1990; NONIA 1963).

But knitting is also an intimate, reflective—and reflexive—activity through which the women of Newfoundland have made sense of their lives, their relationships, and their world. Knitting is about meaning making (Vaccaro 2010); it is a way of theorizing and managing gendered identity, community, and belonging in periods of profound social and economic change, from the grief and loss that accompanied the war (Miller 1916), to the economic and community devastation that followed on the heels of the collapse of the cod fishery in 1992 (Harling Stalker 2006). For

L. Lynda Harling Stalker, women's use of knitting in the aftermath of the cod moratorium can be seen as a manifestation of maternal feminism: "women's work used as a buffer to instability" (2006, 217).

The so-called feminine arts have passed me by. I'm nowhere near an expert quilter. I'm awkward around the sewing machine. I can't always sew in a straight line. The material bunches in funny places. Sometimes the machine won't go at all and then I curse it and all things fabric. But just as Newfoundland's knitters have used needles and yarn to theorize through their stiches, so too does the rhythm of the machine give me room to ponder. Like Phebe Florence Miller's "knitting Marianna" (1916), whose knitting time allows her to reflect on her homefront experiences of war, I have discovered that quilting time is thinking time. Rhythm. Touch. Feel. Sound. Colour. Texture. Routine. All of these work together. My quilting time isn't ever just about the quilt; it is about everything that's rattling around in my brain. Like quilt blocks, ideas, too, can be pieced together, paired up, and squared off, and in that process, new patterns, new linkages, new questions emerge. After several hours together, my fabrics, my thread, and I work not only through a quilt, but also through larger concepts. Together, we massage ideas. Together, we make theory.

In her essay, "Foodmaking as a thoughtful practice," Lisa M. Heldke argues that "[t]he knowing involved in making a cake is 'contained' not simply 'in my head' but in my hands, my wrists, my eyes and nose as well" (1992, 219). Theory, here, is profoundly embodied, located in touch, smell, taste, and the body's memories. Foodmaking, she writes, is "theoretically practical" (1992, 203; see also Heldke 1988). The same might be said of quilting. As I work my quilt through the machine, I consider the potential of quilt making as a space for embodied thinking, processing, knowing. Of making theory in a material sense. What stories can 400 squares tell?

Central to all handcraft is a focus on process. The end result of domestic craft work may be beautiful, but it is the process—the act of making and doing—that matters most (Vaccaro 2010). Handcraft makes meaning through touch. The yarn, the thread, fabric, the stitches—they *are* the story, they *are* the theory. "Quilts, embroideries, and weavings can hold remembrances both personal and collective," writes Leanne Prain, "and artists can use them to create biographies, autobiographies, genealogies, and memorials" (2014, 103). In this way, handcraft becomes a form of life writing, a language for sharing insights into the intimate, vulnerable self (Smith and Watson 2010; see also Chap. 16, later in this volume).

At a conceptual level, quilting might fall into the realm of assemblage theory, or, perhaps, actor network theory, both of which consider how it is that individual elements gain meaning through their ever-shifting encounters with one another. But quilting is explicitly gendered as women's work and this, too, matters. Indeed, the whole idea of *femmage*, a term coined by artists Miriam Schapiro and Melissa Meyer (1978), celebrates women's histories of collage; that is, of making beauty by bringing disparate scraps together (see also Price 2015). And so, as snowdrifts build up outside my window, slowly burying the road, the car, the front door, and inevitably, the shovels, I think about the lowly patchwork quilt and the work that it has done—and continues to do—to make meaning. Who am I, as I cut fabric, thread my needles, and feed my quilt squares through the machine? Who are we, as we run our fingers across the stitches and patterns that result?

[SB]

References

Black, Shannon. 2017. KNIT + RESIST: Placing the pussyhat project in the context of craft activism. *Gender, Place and Culture* 24 (5): 696–710. https://doi.org/10.1080/0966369X.2017.1335292.

Boon, Sonja, and Beth Pentney. 2017. Knitting the feminist self: Craftivism, yarn-bombing and the navigation of feminist spaces. In *Global currents in gender and feminisms: Canadian and international perspectives*, ed. Glenda Tibe Bonifacio, 21–34. Bingley: Emerald Publishing.

Bratich, Jack Z., and Heidi M. Brush. 2011. Fabricating activism: Craft-work, popular culture, gender. *Utopian Studies* 22 (2): 233–260. https://doi.org/10.5325/utopianstudies.22.2.0233.

Chansky, Ricia A. 2010. A stitch in time: Third-wave feminist reclamation of needled imagery. *Journal of Popular Culture* 43 (4): 681–700. https://doi.org/10.1111/j.1540-5931.2010.00765.x.

Clarke, Kyra. 2016. Willful knitting? Contemporary Australian craftivism and feminist hisotries. *Continuum* 30 (3): 298–306. https://doi.org/10.1080/10304312.2016.1166557.

Cullum, Linda. 1995. 'A woman's place': The work of two women's voluntary organizations in Newfoundland, 1934–1941. In *Their lives and times: Women in Newfoundland and Labrador: A collage*, ed. Carmelita McGrath, Marilyn Porter, and Barbara Neis, 93–108. St. John's: Killick Press.

Duley, Tryphena Chancey. 1916. *A pair of grey socks*. St. John's.

Elinor, Gillian, et al., eds. 1987. *Women and craft*. London: Virago.

Fields, Corey D. 2014. Not your grandma's knitting: The role of identity processes in the transformation of cultural practices. *Social Psychology Quarterly* 77 (2): 150–165. https://doi.org/10.1177/0190272514523624.

Greer, Betsy. 2008. *Knitting for good! A guide to creating personal, social, and political change, stitch by stitch*. Boston: Trumpeter.

———, ed. 2014. *Craftivism: The art of craft and activism*. Vancouver: Arsenal Pulp Press.

Groeneveld, Elizabeth. 2010. 'Join the knitting revolution': Third-wave feminist magazine and the politics of domesticity. *Canadian Review of American Studies* 40 (2): 259–277.

Harling Stalker, L. Lynda. 2006. She seeketh wool: Newfoundland women's use of handknitting. In *Weather's edge: Women in Newfoundland and Labrador*, ed. Marilyn Porter, Linda Cullum, and Carmelita McGrath, 209–218. St. John's: Killick Press.

Heldke, Lisa M. 1988. Recipes for theory making. *Hypatia* 3 (2): 15–30. https://doi.org/10.1111/j.1527-2001.1988.tb00066.x.

———. 1992. Foodmaking as a thoughtful practice. In *Cooking, eating, thinking: Transformative philosophies of food*, ed. Deane W. Curtin and Lisa M. Heldke, 203–229. Bloomington and Indianapolis: Indiana University Press.

House, Edgar. 1990. *The way out: The story of NONIA in Newfoundland, 1920–1990*. St. John's: Creative Publishing.

Kelly, Maura. 2014. Knitting as a feminist project? *Women's Studies International Forum* 44: 133–144. https://doi.org/10.1016/j.wsif.2013.10.011.

Luckman, Susan. 2013. The aura of analogue in a digital age: Women's crafts, creative markets and home-based labour after Etsy. *Cultural Studies Review* 19 (1): 249–270.

Miller, Phebe Florence. 1916. The knitting Marianna. In *The distaff*, ed. Mabel W. LeMessurier, 10. St. John's: The Royal Gazette.

Newfoundland Outport Nursing and Industrial Association. 1963. *A short history of NONIA*. St. John's: NONIA Gift Shop.

Parker, Roszika. 2011. *The subversive stitch: Embroidery and the making of the feminine*. London: I.B.Tauris.

Pentney, Beth Ann. 2008. Feminism, activism, and knitting: Are the fibre arts a viable mode for feminist political action? *Thirdspace: A Journal of Feminist Theory and Culture* 8 (1). http://journals.sfu.ca/thirdspace/index.php/journal/article/viewArticle/pentney/210. Accessed 10 Jan 2018.

Prain, Leanne. 2014. *Strange material: Storytelling through textiles*. Vancouver: Arsenal Pulp Press.

Price, Sally. 2015. On femmage. *E-misférica* 12 (1). http://hemisphericinstitute.org/hemi/en/emisferica-121-caribbean-rasanblaj/price. Accessed 28 Dec 2017.

Schapiro, Miriam, and Melissa Meyer. 1978. Waste not want not: An inquiry into what women saved and assembled—FEMMAGE. *Heresies* 1 (4): 66–69.

Smith, Sidonie, and Julia Watson. 2010. *Reading autobiography: A guide for interpreting life narratives.* 2nd ed. Minneapolis: University of Minnesota Press.

Springgay, Stephanie. 2010. Knitting as an aesthetic of civic engagement: Reconceptualizing feminist pedagogy through touch. *Feminist Teacher* 20 (2): 111–123. https://doi.org/10.5406/femteacher.20.2.0111.

Springgay, S., Nikki Hatza, and Sarah O'Donald. 2011. 'Crafting is a luxury that many women cannot afford': Campus knitivism and an aesthetic of civic engagement. *International Journal of Qualitative Studies in Education* 24 (5): 607–613. https://doi.org/10.1080/09518398.2011.600262.

Vaccaro, Jeanne. 2010. Felt matters. *Women & Performance: A Journal of Feminist Theory* 20 (3): 253–266.

———. 2015. Feelings and fractals: Wooly ecologies of transgender matter. *GLQ: A Journal of Lesbian and Gay Studies* 21 (2–3): 273–293. https://doi.org/10.1215/10642684-2843347.

Warren, Gale Denise. 1998. The Patriotic Association of the Women of Newfoundland: 1914–18. *Aspects: A Publication of the Newfoundland Historical Society* 33 (2): 23–32.

———. 2005. Voluntarism and patriotism: Newfoundland women's war work during the First World War. MA Thesis, Memorial University.

Williams, K.A. 2011. 'Old time mem'ry': Contemporary urban craftivism and the politics of doing-it-yourself in postindustrial America. *Utopian Studies* 22 (2): 303–320.

CHAPTER 14

Proximity: Silence

Abstract This chapter draws on the work of Dionne Brand, M. NourbeSe Philip, Zakiyyah Iman Jackson, Eve Tuck, and C. Ree to consider the nature of silence. Starting from the symbol 'O,' this chapter reads silence in relation to silenced histories, diasporic wanderings, interrupted utterances, island spaces, and the ghostly disturbances of the inbetween. Silence, this chapter observes, is encrypted, a site of contestation and possibility, oppression and resistance.

Keywords Silence • Haunting • Memory • Place

"How can nothing be something," Eve Tuck and C. Ree ask (2013, 657)? When I think of nothingness, I think of a void, of space, of the immeasurable. I think, too, of silence—the space between sounds, the suspense between breaths. It's hard to think of nothing; the very act requires thinking of *something*, even in its absence.

In an addendum to their collaborative essay, "A glossary of haunting," Tuck and Ree chronicle the ghosts of settler colonialism through the haunting symbol of the 'O' (2013). That round little symbol—both a letter and number—conveys as much mystery as meaning by its circular contours. And still, as they observe, "Any consideration of O must also consider the void and the circle" (2013, 657). Plotting the journey of 'O' through linguistic and mathematical history, they identify the etymological root of zero as Arabic, represented as a small circle o, and by the word *sifr*. Initially referring to emptiness and space, *sifr*, or *cipher*, began conjuring connotations as encrypted, coded knowledge (Tuck and Ree 2013, 657). It was, they note, both "empty and full, a way to transform in order to conceal, a void masking a presence" (Tuck and Ree 2013, 657). In other words, it was nothing that was very much something. Like the hauntings of O, the ghosts of colonialism are both visible and invisible—what Dionne Brand might describe as "an absent presence" (2001, 21). If we wish to decipher this ghostly code, or the space within the circle, we must search for the stories of silence—the absences, the gaps, the hauntings; we must look for the *something* masked as *nothing*.

Poet and essayist M. NourbeSe Philip, whose work has explored race, gender, and language, also tackles this notion of silence. Indeed, in her poetry collection, *She tries her tongue, her silence softly breaks* (1989), she highlights the correlation between silence, speech, memory, and history. For example, in her poems, "The question of language is the answer to power," and "Testimony stoops to mother tongue," Philip intentionally leaves space after particular words as a way to challenge the fluidity—and authority—of speech (Philip 1989; see also Philip 1997, 124–5, 127). As Carole Boyce Davies points out, in the poem, "Discourse on the logic of language" (1989), Philip writes an intentional stutter over the word 'language' in a way that reflects the historical disruption and oppression of colonialism upon both language and land (Davies 1994, 117; see also Philip 1997, 127). This creative use of structure unsettles the linear flow of her words—intentionally causing us, as readers, "to stumble," "to trip," and "to tie our tongues" (Philip 1997, 127; see also Chap. 20, later in this volume)—a process which works to draw out the relationship between colonial histories of language and the embodiment of silence (Philip 1989; see also Chap. 18, later in this volume).

However, like speech, silence, too, can be disrupted. In Philip's poem "She tries her tongue; her silence softly breaks," language is linked directly to history, and history, to memory. The act of telling one's story has the power to challenge cultural and historical silences (Philip 1989, 98). Much like the blank, white spaces surrounding words on a page, memory surrounds, and forms, our histories—symbiotic, cyclical (Philip 1989, 98; see also Philip 1997). Like the space within the 'O,' Philip's circular imagery makes her wonder whether history can even exist without memory (Philip 1989, 97). Again, by actively using space in her poetry, Philip hints at the gaps and silences of the historical past.

But this is not to suggest that silence is the same as absence. History may well be past, but it is always present, always waiting, always centred (Philip 1989, 98). In an essay reflecting on the relationship between her words on a page, and the blank spaces surrounding them, Philip proclaims, "the silence is and never was silent" (Philip 1997, 125). If we now look to the space within the circle—the space of silence—we see how nothing is not only something, it is actually *everything*.

Similarly tackling colonialism with, and through, poetic writing, Dionne Brand situates silence alongside questions of history, nation, and home in *A map to the Door of No Return: Notes to belonging* (2001). Thinking of silence as a foreign land, Brand imagines other diasporic people, who, like her, sleep restlessly despite the quietude of dawn. Caught between day and night, here and elsewhere, silence becomes a haunting, a ghostly disturbance of inbetweenness, of placelessness (2001, 52–3). As a noisy marker of the "map to the Door of No Return," silence becomes a navigational tool, "circumnavigating absence" in place and time (Brand 2001, 52–3). Like Philip's histories of circles (1989, 96)—and perhaps, like the continuous circle of history—Brand's country of silence is also necessarily centered (2001, 52–3). The foreign country of silence thus becomes a space that is simultaneously empty and full, akin to that mystifying space within the circle. Intriguingly, for Brand, silence can be understood as place; it is not just something, but some*where*.

Philip, too, contemplates the *place* of silence. In her essay collection, *A genealogy of resistance* (1997), she draws out the poetry of silence through the physical space of islands. For Caribbean islands in particular, haunted by the colonial encounter, this land is surrounded not only by water, but by a "history of interruptions" and silences (Philip 1997, 161). She draws attention to this idea of land *surrounded* by water, not only as the "definition eluding definition" of islands, but to emphasize the physical and metaphorical isolation of island life (Philip 1997, 161; see also Brand 2001, 6–13; Nicolson 2007; and Chap. 1, earlier in this volume). The saltwater circumference of the island thus connotes the circular mystery of 'O'; the existence of a land *as* island requires it to be an isolated space, not unlike the space within the circle.

And yet, Philip proposes an alternative to this seemingly finite definition. By writing her story of "islandness," and of "*I-landness*," she is able to reimagine the colonized land of her Caribbean island 'home' not merely as surrounded by water, but rather, as "*floating*" in it (1997, 162–3; italics original). By reimagining and remapping islands through her own words, she is able to conceive of islands beyond the surrounding water, beyond the colonial boundaries of land, sea, and history. Instead, with her own process of writing, her floating *I-land* comes to the surface; it becomes visible, sentient to both the strengths and dangers of the surrounding sea, yet no longer confined, nor defined by it (Philip 1997, 163; italics original).

What happens, then, if we extend our discourse beyond the surrounding waters of the island, and look instead to the land that balances itself *in* the water, aware of its dangers—both material and metaphoric—and existing in its own right? While silence is closely linked with racist and colonial practices, this is not to say that silence is only a result of oppression or of disempowerment (Jackson 2013, 681; Parpart 2010, 1). As Zakiyyah Iman Jackson reminds us, silence must not be equated with the act of not speaking (2013, 675). Like the 'O' and *sifr*, silence is encrypted, an "empty space" that is a site of both contestation and possibility (Jackson 2013, 675). Furthermore, silence, secrecy, and "self-chosen invisibility" have been used by Black women in particular who are confronted with racist and homophobic circumstances (Parpart 2010, 5).

Turning again to Philip's poetry, we can see how silences operate as resistance to colonial rule. She imagines silences as maternal calm, and further, as a precursor to speech and language, representing the *potential* of a mother tongue (1989). Here, silence is not empty; rather it is the transformative moment between mother and child, between past and future, between anguish and language. Silence thus becomes a space not just for resistance, but also for protection and transformation (Parpart 2010, 8). If we look more closely at silence itself, we can begin to see its function as a space of resistance, as agency, as the *I-land* floating in water (Philip 1997). After all, if we focus solely on the seas surrounding land, we might miss the island altogether.

Through the work of Philip and Brand, we can see how silences may be interpreted as a kind of liminal space—a space of unease and possibility. There is an unsettled potential in the pause. Taking a closer look at silences themselves becomes a step towards *breaking* the silences brought about by histories of racial and colonial oppression. How, then, might stories of *I-landness* help us comprehend the ghosts of colonialism in Newfoundland, this place from which I write, this place I call home? What might we learn from the silences in Newfoundland's haunted histories? Can we unsettle 'our' islander identity beyond its oceanic outline (see also Chap. 17)?

Silence does not mean absence. Rather, silences are stories we must search for, (re)claim, and carry with us into the future (see also Chap. 2). Like Tuck and Ree's *sifr*, silence has potential as a secret, political realm of knowledge. If we consider both the circle *and* the space within, maybe then we can begin to decipher silence, to uncover its sounds, its resonances. If we imagine the island as that haunting symbol 'O,' we can choose to look solely at our edges—the tangible, circular lines that seem to delineate the boundaries of our existence—or we can choose to plumb the inner depths of the void—that secret, haunted space within the circle. And once we listen to the stories of silence, perhaps we can begin to see how *nothing* is always *something*.

[LB]

References

Brand, Dionne. 2001. *A map to the Door of No Return: Notes to belonging.* Toronto: Vintage Canada.

Davies, Carole Boyce. 1994. *Black women, writing and identity: Migrations of the subject.* London: Routledge.

Jackson, Zakiyyah Iman. 2013. Animal: New directions in the theorization of race and posthumanism. *Feminist Studies* 39 (3): 669–685.

Nicolson, Adam. 2007. The Islands. *The Geographical Review* 97 (2): 153–164. https://doi.org/10.1111/j.1931-0846.2007.tb00395.x.

Parpart, Jane L. 2010. Choosing silence: Rethinking voice, agency, and women's empowerment. In *Gendered perspectives on international development, #297*, 1–15. East Lansing, MI: Gender, Development, and Globalization Program, Center for Gender in Global Context, Michigan State University.

Philip, M. NourbeSe. 1989. *She tries her tongue, her silence softly breaks.* Charlottetown: Ragweed Press.

———. 1997. *A genealogy of resistance–And other essays.* Toronto: Mercury Press.

Tuck, Eve, and C. Ree. 2013. A glossary of haunting. In *Handbook of autoethnography*, ed. Stacey Holman Jones, Tony E. Adams, and Carolyn Ellis, 639–658. Walnut Grove: Left Coast Press.

CHAPTER 15

Bodies: S/kinships

Abstract This chapter uses skin as a frame for thinking through human/more-than-human kinship relations. Skin, as a contact zone, enables a thinking through not only of one's relationship with place, but also with the non-human beings with which we are entangled. Drawing on the work of Eva Hayward and Enrique Salmón, this chapter asks us to think both creatively and critically about the skin we are in, the contact zone that forms our first encounters with the more-than-human.

Keywords Skin • Jellyfish • Kinship • Entanglement • Climate change

I am twelve years old, and many traces of my skin are left on a hidden beach in my hometown. I run and trip over rocks, falling on my hands and knees. As skin sloughs off and blood pours out of me, I might call the beach my own body archive. In this place, I can endure anything. I am cut into pieces, but I am tough. The beach makes me this way. I imagine myself as having fantastic powers, as a goddess who can manipulate the elements around her. I am continuously drawn to water. Sometimes I am, in fact, a watery creature washed ashore. As I play, I form sensuous connections with the sun, the sea, and the salty air I breathe.

Around me, gelatinous orbs lie, their forms still in multiple textures and sizes. Some appear to have just recently ended up here, others have dried—or fried—to death on the hot, soft, round beach rocks. I am

© The Author(s) 2018
S. Boon et al., *Autoethnography and Feminist Theory at the Water's Edge*, https://doi.org/10.1007/978-3-319-90829-8_15

moved by this form of non-human littering, the affects of jellyfish wash-
ing onto the beach. I gaze down at them and remember the tormenting
sting of a large jelly I experienced a year earlier when I first started swim-
ming in saltwater. In that moment, I was lit up by a brash and jarring
spark. I hated that jelly then, but now I hurt for these around me. I sweat
in the sun, but surely I cannot suffer the same blazing anguish as the
gooey others at my feet.

Now, as an adult, I recognize the queer effects of multispecies encounters and climate change on my body, my life, my skin. A surface, a texture,
and a map, "skin is the key interface between self and other, between the
biological, the psychic, and the social" (Prosser 1998, 65). On the beach,
my skin is part of a contact zone (Pratt 2002) where I, a fleshy body, meet
visible histories of erosion (see Chap. 10) and looming futures of ecological distortion. Like the jellies, I am marked on the beach. I share my body
with it. Skin forms and reforms. In the hot sun, my blonde hair lightens
and my skin starts to brown. Tiny freckles colour my body. The beach
rocks are hot to the touch, and I can't walk around with my shoes off. My
scars glow in the bright sunshine, and sometimes my skin almost smells
burnt.

Historical and life narratives are inscribed in and on skin. As with the
surface of ice (see Chap. 6), the skin of my rural body narrates a playful
migration across landscapes of my island home. My cuts, scars, and freckles tell stories of my engagement with the world. When I was stung by a
jellyfish, its tentacles brushed ever so gently across my skin, and red marks
embellished my legs for a week. Its touch made me both angry and afraid.
But as I look back at the dead jellies on the beach, I am touched in a different way. I am vulnerable with them. They show no signs of life; it is
impossible for me to revive them. I see myself accidentally stepping on
one, causing it to shatter into pieces. Unable to look away, I imagine their
tentacles reaching up for help, but they are just dead skin now.

Eva Hayward has written extensively about the tentacular affects of jellyfish that spread across multiple kinds of flesh. Encountering and forming
carnal connections with jellyfish inside aquariums (2011), analyzing the
captivity and subjection of more-than-human lives (2012), and tracing the
use of jellyfish in transgenic modifications and human consumption (2013
with Lindsay Kelley), she illustrates that humans and jellyfish continuously
and sensuously touch one another in the everyday. We are entangled
(Haraway 2016). When jellyfish wash up onshore, then, is it by reason of

the surging mercy of waves, or is it a deliberate attempt by the ocean to make human others feel sensualities of and sympathies for life—touching, entangled, tenacious?

On the beach, I hurt for the jellies. Unable to distinguish between different layers of skin—epidermis from mesoglea—I am saddened by their dried bodies. I want to place them back in the water to see if they will become squishy again; I cannot imagine how it must feel to be scorched. Scared for my future, I wonder if my life will be threatened the same way as the Earth heats up. Will my skin crack? Will I suffer? Just a child fascinated by nature, I form a critical s/kinship with jellies. Moved by the textures of viscous flesh, I acknowledge my position in an ecological relationship on the beach where humans and oceanic others meet (Hayward 2011). Touched by a different kind, drawn into the closeness of the encounter, I think of these critters, *Cyanea capillata*, Lion's Mane jellies, as kin (Haraway 2016).

Examining Indigenous relations between humans and nature, Enrique Salmón (2000) proposes the concept of kincentric ecology in which viewing more-than-human forms of life as kin reduces ecological subjection and suffering. In so doing, we might form interactions that "enhance and preserve the ecosystem" (2000, 1327). How might I—might we—practice better everyday actions to reflect the coexistence and cohabitation of Earth with many others? If, as Salmón suggests, we are indeed "sharing breath with our relatives" (2000, 1328), what can jellyfish bodies on beaches tell us about ethno-ecologies? Are they aleatory happenings or meaningful oceanic disposals? How do they ask humans to think creatively?

[DJ]

References

Haraway, Donna. 2016. *Staying with the trouble: Making kin in the Chthulucene.* Durham: Duke University Press.

Hayward, Eva. 2011. Ciliated sense. In *Theorizing animals: Re-thinking humani-mal relations,* ed. Nik Taylor and Tania Signal, 255–280. Leiden: Brill.

———. 2012. Sensational jellyfish: Aquarium affects and the matter of immersion. *Differences: A Journal of Feminist Cultural Studies* 23 (5): 161–196. https://doi.org/10.1215/10407391-1892925.

Kelley, Lindsay, and Eva Hayward. 2013. Carnal light. *Parallax* 19 (1): 114–127. https://doi.org/10.1080/13534645.2013.743297.

Pratt, Mary Louise. 2002. The arts of the contact zone. In *Ways of reading: An anthology for writers*, ed. David Bartholomae and Anthony Petrosky, 604–662. Boston: Bedford-St. Martin's.

Prosser, Jay. 1998. *Second skins: The body narratives of transsexuality*. New York: Columbia University Press.

Salmón, Enrique. 2000. Kincentric ecology: Indigenous perceptions of the human-nature relationship. *Ecological Applications* 10 (5): 1327–1332. https://doi.org/10.1890/1051-0761(2000)010[1327:KEIPOT]2.0.CO;2.

PART IV

Longings

CHAPTER 16

Desire: Mummeries

Abstract This chapter searches for trans threads through time, and imagines a historical relationship between the Newfoundland tradition of mummering and trans embodiment. Both are handmade and both rely on the sensuous and textured labour of crafting identity. The handmade thus becomes an evocative site for theory-making, a space to consider the border crossings between flesh, fabric, and identity.

Keywords Mummer • Trans • Embodiment • Corporeality • Handmade • Identity

On November 11, 2014—Remembrance Day—I started my medical transition from male to female with hormone replacement therapy (HRT). Then and now, I feel that my island home, the enveloping 'rock,' isn't yet ready to fully embrace trans ways of being: this place has split me in two and sent me flying. I run, swim, and scatter across the borders of man/woman, rural/urban, earth/ocean.

One month into my journey of crossing hormonal confines, I left St. John's, the city I had nestled down in, and headed back to New World Island, my rural Newfoundland hometown, for Christmas. My family was loving and supportive, but understanding and learning to grow with the uncertain friction that a transition makes felt and visible materialized slowly, in layers, over time.

S. Boon et al., *Autoethnography and Feminist Theory at the Water's Edge*, https://doi.org/10.1007/978-3-319-90829-8_16

Christmas Day revealed its wondrous notions of kinship, and I felt 'at home' again. I laughed, I gave, and I received. Was I longing for something more? On Boxing Day, I celebrated and took part in Newfoundland traditions, marching in the local Mummers Parade with the boy who shaped me as a rural trans girl—my gay best friend through high school, my confidant (my sis), the only other queer-against-the-world I knew when I first started grappling with transition at fifteen. We dressed and disguised ourselves with tablecloths, wigs, glasses, wool socks, and old 'work clothes' from our dads' sheds. We belonged as queer, for once. As trans?

Trans corporeality has been pathologized, scrutinized, and erased by clinical models of trans identity, as well as exploited and misused in Anglo-American feminist theory (Namaste 2000, 2009). Historically, both clinical and feminist approaches to trans studies have been incapable of recognizing the skills, emotions, and struggles of crafting a trans body. But that Christmas as a mummer, I embodied a girl stretching out into her own world, a young woman thrown together from the materials around her.

What John Szwed describes as a form of "open friendship" (1969, 109), mummering is a customary folk practice in which costumed and disguised visitors travel between various houses in a community to eat, drink, party, and play music with accordions and various kinds of percussion, more recently ugly sticks. Mummers dress themselves in an assemblage of fabric, clothing, and other objects pulled from around the house, each fragmented by texture, style, and function. In this way, mummers transpose everyday materials into handmade fashion, and locate and perform within their desired embodiments.

Jeanne Vaccaro sees embodiment as "the material fabric of the body, its surfaces, inscriptions, energies and flows" (2010, 255). Her inquiry into the *handmade* appreciates, measures, and witnesses the sensuous and textured labour of crafting identity (Vaccaro 2015, 276). The handmade recognizes the work of trans corporeality. Like much of trans theorizing, the handmade starts with the material conditions and transpositions of mapping gender on the body. The body is a site, a location, and a space made of parts and affects. Indeed, trans historian Susan Stryker argues that "no place can be more local than the body" (2008a, 38; see also Chap. 19, later in this volume).

Understanding trans bodies as crafted by hand allows me to recognize, for example, the growth or removal of body hair, the thickening and lengthening of vocal cords from the administration of testosterone, the development of muscle from steroids, estrogen-induced thinning of skin, stretch marks developing on growing breasts, hips and thighs; lip injections and fillers, self-harm scars, imagined modifications, non-operative bodies, and all the surgical procedures and textures of 'cut' life (Hayward 2008, 2010, 2017). Thinking *about*, *with*, and *through* the changing contours of the body (Ahmed and Stacey 2001), those of us who find validation in learning to see trans identities as handmade may recognize how 'skin' in many forms and layers—fabric, hair, tissue—"is attributed a meaning and logic of its own" (Ahmed and Stacey 2001, 3). Envisioning mummers as creative and experimental actors in the making of island trans history, I illustrate a textured assemblage of time, tradition, and touch. Further, imagining mummer costumes as kinds of skin, and trans embodiment as an enfolded (Carter 2013) re-fashioning of the body, I open up space for analyzing the labour of what and how 'trans' unfolds over time in Newfoundland.

Making theory at the interplay of flesh and fabric (Vaccaro 2015, 275), many mummers disguise themselves across gendered borders (Szwed 1969; Jarvis 2014). Although scholars have used the term "cross-dressing" to describe mummer bodies, I want to intentionally avoid this designation in order to conceptualize mummering instead as a form of drag, a handmade gender performance (Butler 1990). Geopolitical in nature, Newfoundland mummer drag subverts rural struggle and hard labour into a fluid and performative figuration of family, community, and gender alterity. As Rosi Braidotti suggests, "figurations are not figurative ways of thinking, but rather more materialistic mappings of situated, or embedded and embodied, positions" (2002, 2). Because trans experiences have been historically and intimately connected to drag identity and performance (Stryker 2008b), perhaps then, trans forms of being have not been historically silenced in Newfoundland; rather, trans murmurs have been figured and handcrafted—being heard, seen, and felt over time.

As a mummering body embellished with an oil-stained flannel, floral tights with foam pads stuffed inside, and an old doily table cloth thrown over my face, I am allowed to transgress the borders of old and new, man and woman, young and aging. Past, present, and future are torn (see Chap. 19) and tangle into each other through stitches and rips in fabric as an ugly stick thumps against the ground. Sewn together anew from recycled threads, they form something that cannot be forgotten, cannot be erased. In this moment as mummer, like all other moments of my life now as trans, "I am an act of kneading" (Anzaldúa 2012, 103). This moment is about process, making, undoing, folding (see also Chaps. 13 and 19). But before I know it, the Mummers Parade is over. I strip myself out of my creation, knowing that I cannot live my life as a mummer; it wouldn't be acceptable. Mummering is play; it isn't 'real.' However, the figuration of the mummer never fully leaves. Although I remove the ornaments, the mummer remains as a cultural commodity, a visitor, a friend.

Recognizing the ontological imbrication of mummer and trans, I am unsettled by the language used to describe bodies like ours: costume, cross-dressing, foolishness. I acknowledge how costumes are considered artificial, how 'drag' has been constructed as a form of imitation and inter-pretation, 'trans' as a deceptive identity. The complex interplay between dress, flesh, and subjectivity has not been taken seriously as a form of crossing/permeating gender or skin. Rather, as Jay Prosser suggests, ideas about costumes are connected to stereotypes about trans bodies, in which "that figure of the body as costume is surely welded most firmly to the transsexual" (1998, 62) in order to deny us legal protections, health care, and employment (Namaste 2009). Yes, mummering—this form of art that moves me to write through my life—is costumed, but most significantly it demonstrates a political display of living across borders, of enfolding and emotional geographies, no matter how difficult to cross.

Mummer costumes also transpose the material footing of rural island lives. An assemblage of objects and emotions, mummer costumes can be understood as vibrant matter (Bennett 2010). Still, some believe that their 'parts' or skins carry no meaning, that they are 'useless' (Sellars 2008). How can I make theory with mummers? Asking this question through skin, the trans figure—the mummer—might be read as a *'woolage,'* a Newfoundland vernacular term for an individual with unkempt hair (imag-ine a wig or mop head), who produces affects in and forms a haptic con-nection with me. Most significantly, this figure is a symbol of the deteriorative flow (wool-age) of fibrous difference, of strands and tissues being pulled apart to open up possibilities for the future (see Chap. 19).

Now I caress, press against, hold on to the memories, or "mummeries" (Power 2015, A4) of the Parade, with these thoughts in my head: What if mummers in Newfoundland have been crafting and embodying trans identity all along, making political noise with an ugly stick even before trans as a state of gendered shifting, growing, and becoming in Newfoundland was discursively produced? Are current textures of trans life in Newfoundland haunted by mummers (Tuck and Ree 2013)? In what ways might the performance of trans-through-time in Newfoundland be *felt*? (Million 2009; Paterson 2005; Vaccaro 2010).

Eve Kosofsky Sedgwick argues that "the definition of performativity itself is inflected by the language of texture" (2003, 16). Like wool fibers scattered throughout a mummer costume, rubbing against the disguised and dressed body, and against other forms of fabric, trans presents in Newfoundland create friction with coarse visions of the past. And like beer caps on a broom handle—an ugly stick thumping against the ground—trans presence makes noise in creative ways, sending out tender and sensational vibrations of activist labour, gender diversity, and social change. Vaccaro suggests that the handmade recognizes trans lives as experimental (2015, 277). Thus, the handmade situates trans ontology as a kind of invention, a process of affective-embodied-performative-temporal-textured mosaic-making. Indeed, mummers have always exhibited mosaic and inventive assemblages.

Like generating new layers of skin, I write a convergence of overlapping positions: drag, trans, mummer, performance, identity, figure, figuration, subject, object, spectacle, individual. I do not wish to seek out clearly defined spaces between trans and drag, between trans and mummer or subject and object, but rather ask after what lies in the hyphenated zones that touch many of these positions at the same time (Wah 2006). Witnessing the interplay of flesh and fabric—reading trans as mummer or mummer as trans, trans as object, trans as spectacle—allows me to ask, following Sara Ahmed, "how do bodies 'matter' in what objects do" (2006, 51)? What does a trans woman mummer say about the customary art? Is she un/doing gender, twice (Butler 1990)? Is she adding more layers to complicate the potential of trans as fabrication, as figuration, as movement, as performance—through the body alone? Does mummering represent a form of trans life that is less vulnerable—less of a zoetic translation—than a fleshy shifting of gender or sex?

Stretching out fingers to feel the handmade textures of my mummer costume pulls me through history. As I look for trans threads through time, I understand more clearly what Jay Prosser means when he writes: "the body of transsexual becoming is born out of a yearning for a perfect past—that is, not memory but nostalgia" (1998, 84). With all of this at my fingertips, and treasuring my mummeries of handmade trans ontologies in Newfoundland, it is possible that my belonging as a trans woman islander has been stitched together slowly and queerly over generations by mummers near and far. As I reach back to acknowledge and thank them, I look forward into pastpresent (Hayward 2010) island life, where bodies of shifting sorts, skins, and mosaic surfaces rub against each other—haunting, hemming, hyphening.

[DJ]

REFERENCES

Ahmed, Sara. 2006. *Queer phenomenology: Orientations, objects, others*. Durham and London: Duke University Press.

Ahmed, Sara, and Jackie Stacey, eds. 2001. *Thinking through the skin*. London and New York: Routledge.

Anzaldúa, Gloria. 2012. *Borderlands/La frontera: The new Mestiza*. 4th ed. San Francisco: Aunt Lute Books.

Bennett, Jane. 2010. *Vibrant matter: A political ecology of things*. Durham: Duke University Press.

Braidotti, Rosi. 2002. *Metamorphoses: Towards a materialist theory of becoming*. Cambridge: Polity Press.

Butler, Judith. 1990. *Gender trouble: Feminism and the subversion of identity*. New York: Routledge.

Carter, Julian. 2013. Embracing transition, or dancing in the folds of time. In *The transgender studies reader 2*, ed. Susan Stryker and Aren Aizura, 130–144. New York: Routledge.

Hayward, Eva. 2008. More lessons from a starfish: Prefixial flesh and transspeciated selves. *Women's Studies Quarterly* 36 (3–4): 64–85. https://doi.org/10.1353/wsq.0.0099.

———. 2010. Spider city sex. *Women & Performance: A Journal of Feminist Theory* 20 (3): 225–251. https://doi.org/10.1080/0740770X.2010.529244.

———. 2017. Don't exist. *TSQ: Transgender Studies Quarterly* 4 (2): 191–194. https://doi.org/10.1215/23289252-3814985.

Jarvis, Dale. 2014. *Any mummers 'lowed in?: Christmas mummering traditions in Newfoundland and Labrador*. St. John's: Flanker Press.

Million, Dian. 2009. Felt theory: An Indigenous feminist approach to affect and history. *Wicazo Sa Review* 24 (2): 53–76. https://doi.org/10.1353/wic.0.0043.

Namaste, Viviane. 2000. Access denied: The experience of transsexuals and transgendered people with health care and social services in Toronto. In *Invisible lives: The erasure of transsexual and transgendered people*, 157–189. Chicago and London: University of Chicago Press.

———. 2009. Undoing theory: The 'transgender question' and the epistemic violence of Anglo-American feminist theory. *Hypatia* 24 (3): 11–32. https://doi.org/10.1111/j.1527-2001.2009.01043.x.

Paterson, Mark. 2005. Affective touch: Towards a 'felt' phenomenology of therapeutic touch. In *Emotional geographies*, ed. Joyce Davidson, Liz Bondi, and Mick Smith, 161–176. New York and London: Routledge.

Power, Louis. 2015. Making mummeries. *The Telegram*, December 21.

Prosser, Jay. 1998. *Second skins: The body narratives of transsexuality*. New York: Columbia University Press.

Sedgwick, Eve Kosofsky. 2003. *Touching feeling: Affect, pedagogy, performativity.* Durham and London: Duke University Press.

Sellars, Jason. 2008. DIY: Ugly stick. *The Scope*, July 3.

Stryker, Susan. 2008a. Dungeon intimacies: The poetics of transsexual sadomasochism. *Parallax* 14 (1): 36–47. https://doi.org/10.1080/13534640701781362.

———. 2008b. Transgender history, homonormativity, and disciplinarity. *Radical History Review* 100: 145–157. https://doi.org/10.1215/01636545-2007-026.

Szwed, John. 1969. The mask of friendship: Mumming as a ritual of social relations. In *Christmas Mumming in Newfoundland*, ed. Herbert Halpert and G.M. Story, 104–118. Toronto: University of Toronto Press.

Tuck, Eve, and C. Ree. 2013. A glossary of haunting. In *Handbook of autoethnography*, ed. Stacey Holman Jones, Tony E. Adams, and Carolyn Ellis, 639–658. Walnut Grove: Left Coast Press.

Vaccaro, Jeanne. 2010. Felt matters. *Women & Performance: A Journal of Feminist Theory* 20 (3): 253–266. https://doi.org/10.1080/0740770X.2010.529245.

———. 2015. Feelings and fractals: Wooly ecologies of transgender matter. *GLQ: A Journal of Lesbian and Gay Studies* 21 (2–3): 273–293. https://doi.org/10.1215/10642684-2843347.

Wah, Fred. 2006. *Diamond grill.* Edmonton: NeWest Press.

CHAPTER 17

Home: Islandness

Abstract Reflecting on experiences of homesickness, this chapter explores ideas of longing, home, place, and identity through encounters with land and sea. It interrogates islandness and island identity, looking in particular at the intricate dynamics of colonialism, history, and belonging in Newfoundland. Following the work of Vicki Hallett, Jennifer Bowering Delisle, Ursula Kelly, and Susan M. Manning, this chapter highlights Indigenous histories in an effort to challenge Newfoundlanders' white settler identity, which relies on the active erasure of long Indigenous presence on the island, and on settler claims to indigeneity. This chapter argues for a more complicated engagement with island identity, one that is attentive to the complex relationships between past, present, and future.

Keywords Islandness • Identity • Belonging • Colonialism • Self-indigenization

By the time I reached the final year of my undergraduate degree, many of my friends had already moved away from Newfoundland to pursue work and further postsecondary education. On social media, they would share pictures, articles, and videos that highlighted the charm and eccentricity of our island. I was particularly amused at how many of them suddenly started

S. Boon et al., *Autoethnography and Feminist Theory at the Water's Edge*, https://doi.org/10.1007/978-3-319-90829-8_17

using images of St. John's harbour on their profile pages. Convinced that this nostalgic display of our island was fueled merely by homesickness and a desire to show non-Newfoundlanders the unique and "quirky" nature of this place (McDonald 2006, 15), I vowed I would never let nostalgia cloud what I perceived as the mediocre reality of my island home. The grass, after all, is usually greener on the other side.

But all of this changed when I moved to Manchester, England, for graduate school. With the Atlantic Ocean now between my home and me—from one island to another—I soon realized I was not immune from those same longings. Although I loved Manchester, there was something about that grey, industrial city that made me appreciate the colourful and charismatic city I called home. And so, despite resisting the temptation for a few months, I too, like many expats before me, found myself uploading an image of the St. John's waterfront to my Facebook page. Still aware of the romanticization that this nostalgia could breed, I captioned it with: "St. John's harbour: the quintessential cover photo for expats." Somehow, I hoped that the irony would salvage my blatant homesickness.

Perhaps unsurprisingly, it wasn't until my time away from Newfoundland that I began to really tackle the complexities of my foggy, islander identity (see Chaps. 6 and 9, earlier in this volume, and Kelly 2009, 36). Indeed, as John Gillis suggests, "[w]hen it comes to islands, absence makes the heart grow fonder" (2007, 282). What was it about my island home that captivated me so, despite my best intentions? Why did something as silly as a Facebook picture feel like such a powerful representation of identity, of islandness? It would be easy to deem these details trivial, but as Ursula Kelly writes, "the minutiae of our lives are saturated with meaning" (2009, 33). It is through these seemingly insignificant stories of life that we find meaning and insight. Minutiae, in this sense, becomes "monumental" (Kelly 2009, 33).

If we think of islandness through the minutiae of affect or feeling, we can begin to examine more critically the connections between our selves and our islands (Vannini and Taggart 2012, 236; see also Conkling 2007). Phillip Vannini and Jonathan Taggart suggest that islandness is shaped by the ways we "dwell" on our island, or how we "understand and appreciate its sounds, sights, textures, flavors, and scents" (2012, 236; see also Chaps. 7 and 9, earlier in this volume). Islanders and islands are thus implicated in a mutual becoming of body and place (Vannini and Taggart 2012, 237), a transformation, in a way, from islandness, to "*I-landness*" (Philip 1997, 163; italics original). How then, do I understand, and become with, the island I call home? How do I articulate, and make sense of, this pervasive longing for the St. John's waterfront?

Perhaps the power of this place rests in the very essence of its islandness—a contact zone where water meets land, and where cultures clash (Pratt 2002; see also Hallett 2016). Island/ness, in this sense, becomes a kind of border/land (Anzaldúa 2012; see also Olwig 2007)—"complex, multifaceted, muddy" (Hallett 2016, para. 4). But, as 'we' claim this island as home, who is included, and who is excluded, from the borders of be/longing (Kelly 2009, 35)? What is implicated in this longing for an island, for a home?

Those who write about what it means to be a Newfoundlander often discuss the "troubling" and "complicated" process of identity making (Tilley 2010; Hallett 2010; see also Buss/Clarke 1999; Delisle 2008; Kelly 2009; Manning 2017). While Susan Tilley writes of an identity grounded in the "concrete, material land and sea" and a home that is geographically fixed (2010, 127–8), other islanders are more critical of this reliance on the fixed and physical for identity formation. For example, while Vicki Hallett (2010) and Daze Jefferies (Chap. 9) acknowledge the undeniable influence of the landscape on Newfoundland identity, due in large part to the historical prominence of the fishery, they also remind us that there are many factors in play beyond the purely physical. Indeed, feminist geographers remind me that places are "contested, fluid, and uncertain" (McDowell qtd. in Hallett 2010, 76; see also Goeman 2013). Ursula Kelly similarly warns that "[g]eographies are sites onto which we may manifest our longing, but they cannot contain or fully assuage them" (2009, 36). The place of home, in particular, is a thorny composite of politics and mythology; home is "a fiction fraught with contradictions," and yet, it is also a fiction in which we live (Kelly 2009, 36; see also Brand 2001; Gillis 2007; Wah 2006). What is it that I long for as an islander? What does 'home' entail?

One day, I decided to take a spontaneous day trip to Liverpool, a short 45-minute train ride from Manchester. It was raining in Manchester, as it often does, and I needed a change of scenery. I wasn't expecting to ease my homesickness, and yet, walking down Liverpool's Church Street, a popular pedestrian shopping area, I was suddenly struck by a familiar sound: seagulls. Seagulls aren't exactly novel when you grow up by the ocean; in fact, they are so ordinary that they are more likely to be perceived as a nuisance than as grounds for nostalgia. But after living in a city in which the hiss and hum of a seemingly endless line of buses was the most characteristic sound, the screech of seagulls suddenly seemed symphonic.

I kept walking until I reached the waterfront, where I was greeted with the pleasant sight of docks and ships bobbing along with the River Mersey's calm, glistening waves. The Mersey is very different from the rugged, salt-water coasts of Newfoundland, but still, it reminded me of the dewy, sea air, foggy horizons, and the lilting waves characteristic of the St. John's water-front. Water, I suddenly realized, had the power to flood my body, my memory, and my self with feelings of home (see Chap. 8). Indeed, the presence of the sea was one constant in Newfoundland, a place that otherwise seemed to be ever changing: be it culturally, politically, or economically (Buss/Clarke 1999; Delisle 2008, 2013; Hallett 2010; Kelly 2009; Tilley 2010).

However, as I took a closer look at the buildings lining Liverpool's Albert Dock, I noticed one in particular that seemed to unsettle the serenity of the landscape. The International Slavery Museum, tucked alongside the Tate Liverpool Art Gallery and the Beatles Story Museum, helped keep my nostalgia in check. I began thinking about the darker histories of the waterfront, the ones I had forgotten in my sentimental encounter with the River Mersey. What other stories did these shores tell? What other emotions might the sea incite (Alexander 2006; Walcott 2007)? And what about my relationship with the waterfront that I called home? What histories existed beyond the brightly coloured buildings and muddy waters that line the St. John's waterfront? Further, what efforts do Newfoundlanders make to acknowledge our own difficult pasts? Who is left out of our idealized view of Newfoundland identity, the one captured in sunny photos of St John's harbour?

While having a sense of Newfoundland identity is not problematic in itself, it becomes so when it is founded on a colonial myth of patrilineal purity. Vicki Hallett (2016), an islander herself, examines how popular narratives tend to portray white settler Newfoundlanders as being deeply rooted to the land and sea, as though they have always been born to this island. Such representations mythologize settler masculinities through acts of self-indigenization (2016, para. 2; see also McDonald 2006). This kind of cultural origin story represents Newfoundlanders as not only "having an indigenized culture, but *as* indigenous people" (2016, para. 8, italics added; see also Delisle 2006; Goldie 1992), an approach that both disregards histories of colonial violence and appropriates what it means to be 'native' to the island (Delisle 2006, 37; see also Manning 2017). As the majority of those who claim to be Newfoundlanders are descendants of European settlers, this process of indigenization works to affirm white settler identities through the collective erasure of actual Indigenous identities from the island (Delisle 2006; Kelly 2009; Manning 2017; see also McDonald 2006).

Susan M. Manning reminds us that the island of Newfoundland, known as Ktaqmkuk, or "across the waves/water" in the Mi'kmaw language, is the longstanding territory of the Mi'kmaq and Beothuk people (2017, 1). However, this reality is often left out of popular stories of the island (Manning 2017, 1). Manning further suggests that dominant histories of Newfoundland and Labrador perpetuate its own "marginalised place" within Canadian Confederation, a narrative which selectively blurs and buries real stories of settler colonialism within the province (Manning 2017, 1–4; see also Delisle 2006, 2008). As such, it is by challenging and "(re)storying" these narrative myths and silences (see Chap. 14) within Newfoundland's dominant history that we can effectively work towards decolonisation on this island (Manning 2017, 5; see also Chaps. 7 and 16, earlier in this volume). Although islanders may feel as though their identity is deeply rooted in the physical landscape of this place, identity and landscape are not fixed or devoid of political meaning. After all, the very act of claiming a land as home is political in and of itself.

What really makes an islander? Is it in the body? Is it in the mind? Is it in the water? The land? And at what point can one *become* a Newfoundlander, if at all (see Chap. 20)? Clearly, what constitutes a Newfoundlander is becoming increasingly complex. Or maybe it has always been complex, and only now are we beginning to see through the clouds of colonial nostalgia and sift through our muddied pasts.

[LB]

REFERENCES

Alexander, M. Jacqui. 2006. *Pedagogies of crossing: Meditations on feminism, sexual politics, memory, and the sacred*. Durham: Duke University Press.

Anzaldúa, Gloria. 2012. *Borderlands/La frontera: The new mestiza*. 4th ed. San Francisco: Aunt Lute Books.

Brand, Dionne. 2001. *A map to the Door of No Return: Notes to belonging*. Toronto: Vintage Canada.

Buss, Helen M./ Margaret Clarke. 1999. *Memoirs from away: A new found land girlhood*. Waterloo: Wilfred Laurier University Press.

Conkling, Philip. 2007. On islanders and islandness. *The Geographical Review* 97 (2): 191–201. https://doi.org/10.1111/j.1931-0846.2007.tb00398.x.

Delisle, Jennifer Bowering. 2006. Nation, indigenization, the Beothuk: A Newfoundland myth of origin in Patrick Kavanagh's *Gaff topsails*. *Studies in Canadian Literature/Études en littérature canadienne* 31 (2): 23–45.

————. 2008. A Newfoundland diaspora?: Moving through ethnicity and whiteness. *Canadian Literature* 196: 64–81.

————. 2013. *The Newfoundland diaspora: Mapping the literature of out-migration.* Waterloo: Wilfrid Laurier University Press.

Gillis, John R. 2007. Island sojourns. *The Geographical Review* 97 (2): 274–287. https://doi.org/10.1111/j.1931-0846.2007.tb00403.x.

Goeman, Mishuana. 2013. *Mark my words: Native women mapping our nations.* Minneapolis: University of Minnesota.

Goldie, Terry. 1992. The man of the land/the land of the man: Patrick White and Scott Symons. *SPAN* 36. http://wwwmcc.murdoch.edu.au/ReadingRoom/litserv/SPAN/36/Goldie.html. Accessed 25 Aug 2017.

Hallett, Vicki. 2010. Continuous erosion: Place and identity in the lives of Newfoundland women. In *Despite this loss: Essays on culture, memory and identity in Newfoundland and Labrador,* ed. Ursula A. Kelly and Elizabeth Yeoman, 74–90. St. John's: ISER Books.

————. 2016. Cold water cowboys and Newfoundland masculinity. *Acadiensis.* https://acadiensis.wordpress.com/2016/06/13/cold-water-cowboys-and-newfoundland-masculinity/. Accessed 25 Aug 2017.

Kelly, Ursula. 2009. *Migration and education in a multicultural world: Culture, loss, and identity.* New York: Palgrave Macmillan.

Manning, Susan M. 2017. Contrasting colonisations: (Re)storying Newfoundland/Ktaqmkuk as place. *Settler Colonial Studies.* Online First. https://doi.org/10.1080/2201473X.2017.1327010.

McDonald, Terry. 2006. Proud to be an islander: Newfoundland identity as revealed through Newfoundland song. *Canadian Folk Music Bulletin* 40 (2): 15–22.

Olwig, Karen Fog. 2007. Islands as places of being and belonging. *The Geographical Review* 97 (2): 260–273. https://doi.org/10.1111/j.1931-0846.2007.tb00402.x.

Philip, M. NourbeSe. 1997. *A genealogy of resistance–And other essays.* Toronto: Mercury Press.

Pratt, Mary Louise. 2002. The arts of the contact zone. In *Ways of reading: An anthology for writers,* ed. David Bartholomae and Anthony Petrosky, 604–662. Boston: Bedford-St. Martin's.

Tilley, Susan. 2010. Re-searching ties to home: 'Troubling' notions of identity. In *Despite this loss: Essays on culture, memory and identity in Newfoundland and Labrador,* ed. Ursula A. Kelly and Elizabeth Yeoman, 127–136. St. John's: ISER Books.

Vannini, Phillip, and Jonathan Taggart. 2012. Doing islandness: A non-representational approach to an island's sense of place. *Cultural Geographies* 20 (2): 225–242. https://doi.org/10.1177/1474474011428098.

Wah, Fred. 2006. *Diamond grill.* Edmonton: NeWest Press.

Walcott, Derek. 2007. *Selected poems.* London: Farrar, Straus & Giroux.

CHAPTER 18

Vulnerability: Refusal

Abstract At heart a meditation on methodology, this chapter considers the relationships between ethics and colonial archives. Drawing on recent work by Quinn Eades, Saidiya Hartman, Katherine McKittrick, Elspeth Probyn, Eve Tuck, and K. Wayne Yang, among others, and considering the writing of poet and essayist M. NourbeSe Philip, it assesses the potential of ethnographic refusal as a way of reading the violence of the colonial archive differently.

Keywords Refusal • Archives • Ethics • Vulnerability • Skin

I never expected to find my ancestors in Newfoundland, and so I never thought to look for them. Why would I? I've learned my place. I am, in local parlance, a Come From Away, a Mainlander, someone who makes home here only by chance. My body, my self aren't rooted to this rock in the Atlantic; rather, they've just appeared here. I have no family here, no history, no culture. I am a transient—a Newfoundlander only by convenience—and on this windswept rock, this matters.

On the surface, Newfoundland seems far removed from the Dutch colonial histories that hold my pasts. It's a lonely, brooding island in the North Atlantic. But this island's economic fortunes are fully embedded in imperial histories. Newfoundland salt cod has travelled the globe, linking European wealth with Caribbean slavery and indenture (Janzen 2008; see

© The Author(s) 2018
S. Boon et al., *Autoethnography and Feminist Theory at the Water's Edge*, https://doi.org/10.1007/978-3-319-90829-8_18

also Snooks and Boon 2017). The Maritime History Archive, housed on our university campus, meanwhile, is a colonial treasure trove: it holds fully 75% of all the Crew Agreements and Ship's Logs of all British-registered ships sailing between 1857 and 1942 (Maritime History Archive 2015). Among them are the records for the Kate Kellock, a Liverpool-based ship that transported emigrants—including two of my own ancestors—from what was then Calcutta to Paramaribo, Suriname, to work as indentured labourers on Surinamese sugar, coffee, and cotton plantations.

Britain. India. Suriname. Newfoundland. Imagine my surprise when I discovered that our histories—Newfoundland's and mine—were not, in the end, all that different. In fact, they are deeply interwoven (Snooks and Boon 2017; see also Braidotti 2011, 2014).

Ships' Logs reveal details about emigrant births and deaths, illnesses and sufferings during long oceanic journeys. They also tell stories of the often fraught relationships between seamen and the human cargo they were transporting. These Logs are among the only records that remain of those who travelled more than halfway around the world to work on contract in Caribbean plantations; they are the only documents on which families and researchers might draw in order to recover their histories. And yet, read as a unit, they also contribute to a dismembering—and, indeed, dehumanizing—of the colonized body. Is it possible to re-member (de Vries 2004) the past differently? More provocative still, although some of these records concern my own family histories, what right do I have to tell these stories, even if they are the "very [me] of [me]" (Tuck & Yang 2014a, 234)?

My musings here are born of a methodological quandary: how can I research in and write about colonial archives—whose contents include the stories of my own ancestors—without contributing to and/or perpetuating the violence that they enact (Hartman 2008; McKittrick 2014)? In her 2001 essay, "Eating skin," Elspeth Probyn offers a searching and probing meditation on skin, both the skin we inhabit and that which we desire. Like Probyn, I am a researcher who longs for skin, the skin of my histories, of my ancestors (see also Chaps. 2 and 19). The stories inscribed on, in, and through their bodies. But is my longing an ethical longing? Although these are my histories, my pasts, my stories, and my skins, do I have a right to tell them, to explore them, to expose them? What will I do with the archival data that I gather? What does it mean? How might I tell this tangled story of indenture?

Nineteenth-century paper is fragile, prone to crumbling. Pulpy and thick, it lacks the elegance of the linen-rich paper from earlier centuries. And so, as I pull the Ship's Log toward me, I am gentle, as gentle as I can be; if these stories disappear, they're gone forever (see also Chap. 19). Seared with sea salt and time, the papers won't lie flat, and so the document lies awkwardly on the table, an origami animal gone wrong. To read it, I need to angle my head, first one way and then the other. Even then, some words remain distorted, lost in time.

Why, in the end, am I at the Maritime History Archive anyway? Is it about lofty scholarly visions of transnational histories and global identities? Or is it about consumption, about a desire to "eat the Other" (hooks 1992), to assimilate the flesh and bones of my ancestors into my own body? In the Ship's Logs, I am searching for skin, for *my* skin. The skin that is mine and not mine. The skin that I have never lived, but that has imprinted itself on my pasts and lives on in the DNA of my presents. The skin that tells itself only in colonial records that mark every detail, every body part, that dismember that skin, that open the body, wound it, and reconstruct it for the colonial gaze. In the archives, I'm searching for the skin I'm in, the chameleon skin that almost passes. Not quite. White.

"Aren't we all implicated in each other?" Dionne Brand asks (2001, 166). "We are undone by each other," Judith Butler affirms (2004, 19). Undone and made so vulnerable we cannot *not* be undone. In eating the skin of the archive, I am consuming my own flesh, a carnivore self-cannibalizing my histories, a parasite in search of my pasts.

Come from away. Mainlander. Who am I on this island? Who am I in this place? Where is away? Where is the mainland? Where do I belong? What story can I tell here? I lose my footing, tangling myself into impossibilities. I tumble into the data, tripping, falling, my skin bruised and scraped, a wound bursting open. "This is what happens when we try to dig out trauma: we take memory and narrative with it. We take desire. We take love," Quinn Eades counsels me (2015, 128). Perhaps this wounding is necessary; perhaps my archival undoing is essential. Perhaps this tangle is the price of an ethical encounter.

Where can this story begin? Can it begin at all? Not all stories, Eve Tuck and K. Wayne Yang argue, should be told. Not all stories have a right to be told: "Tissue samples, blood draws, and cheek swabs are not only our own," Tuck and Ree write, "the DNA contained in them is shared by our relatives, our ancestors, our future generations .... This is equally true of stories" (2014a, 233–4). But if, as Saidiya Hartman has argued, stories might be understood as "a form of compensation or even as reparations" (2008, 4), then what choices do we have? How do we move forward? How can we approach the archive differently, when archival dismemberings are the only traces that remain? What other stories can these materials tell, and how might we equip ourselves to listen for them?

Tuck and Yang propose a model of ethnographic refusal, an approach to writing and researching that, in their words, "shifts the gaze from the violated body to the violating instruments" (2014a, 241). Such an approach allows researchers to focus on the larger structure of violence (2014a, 241; see also 2014b). One example of this process might be found in the work of M. NourbeSe Philip. A lawyer, essayist, and poet born in Tobago and living in Toronto, Philip refuses colonial logic in all of her writing (see Chap. 14). *Zong!*, published in 2011, is her poetic re-writing of the Gregson v. Gilbert court case, the only written document pertaining to the 1781 killing of some 150 enslaved Africans who were ordered to be thrown overboard from the slave ship, *Zong*, for insurance monies. *Zong!* is constructed entirely from the court transcript of the trial. "There is," Philip writes in the essay that accompanies the poems, "no telling this story" (2011, 196). And so instead, she *undoes* the story, reducing the violence of the colonial text to sounds, rhythms, spaces. Staging the fragments across the page, Philip imagines waves and oceans, the individual sounds and letters floating against, beyond, and through one another in the carnage of transatlantic slavery. This poetic deconstruction and reconstruction not only *resists* logic, but confounds it altogether.

Like Tuck and Yang, Philip performs refusal. She will not tell the story that the court case has determined for her; rather, she engages in a much more subversive project, a 'not-telling' that, in its telling, challenges the very nature of logic itself (2011, 197). Philip suggests that none of us is innocent; we are all implicated in the violence that begot the massacre on the *Zong*. As soon as we engage with the text, as soon as we struggle with it, we become part of it (Philip 2011, 198). There is no escape. A politics of refusal, then, entangles us in the discomfort of the very text we seek to resist.

"I want to know how to eat skin, the skin of the other; to eat skin well, to hope for my skin to be well eaten," writes Elspeth Probyn (2001, 91). As I sit in the Maritime History Archive, Ship's Logs spread out before me and the taste of salt cod on my tongue, I wonder about the relationship between longing and belonging. I wonder about dismembering and remembering and I wonder what it might mean to eat skin well. Is it possible to eat the other without consuming them? Or might a new way of eating the other—a palate haunted by the presence of the past—offer another way of refusing research?

[SB]

REFERENCES

Braidotti, Rosi. 2011. *Nomadic subjects: Embodiment and sexual difference in contemporary feminist theory.* 2nd ed. New York: Columbia University Press.

———. 2014. Writing as a nomadic subject. *Comparative Critical Studies* 11 (2–3): 163–184. https://doi.org/10.3366/ccs.2014.0122.

Brand, Dionne. 2001. *A map to the Door of No Return: Notes to belonging.* Toronto: Vintage Canada.

Butler, Judith. 2004. *Undoing gender.* New York and London: Routledge.

de Vries, Maggie. 2004. *Missing Sarah: A memoir of loss.* Toronto: Penguin Canada.

Eades, Quinn. 2015. *All the beginnings: A queer autobiography of the body.* North Melbourne: Tantanoola.

Hartman, Saidiya. 2008. Venus in two acts. *Small Axe* 12 (2): 1–14. https://doi.org/10.2979/SAX.2008.-.26.1.

hooks, bell. 1992. Eating the other: Desire and resistance. In *Black looks: Race and representation,* 21–39. Boston: South End Press.

Janzen, Olaf U. 2008. The 'long' eighteenth century, 1697–1815. In *A short history of Newfoundland and Labrador,* ed. Newfoundland Historical Society, 49–76. St. John's: Newfoundland Historical Society.

Maritime History Archive. 2015. Crew list index search. https://www.mun.ca/mha/holdings/searchcombinedcrews.php. Accessed 20 Mar 2018.

McKittrick, Katherine. 2014. Mathematics Black life. *The Black Scholar* 44 (2): 16–28. https://doi.org/10.1080/00064246.2014.11413684.

Philip, M. NourbeSe. 2011. *Zong!* Middletown: Wesleyan University Press.

Probyn, Elspeth. 2001. Eating skin. In *Thinking through the skin,* ed. Sara Ahmed and Jackie Stacey, 87–103. London and New York: Routledge.

Snooks, Gina, and Sonja Boon. 2017. Salt fish and molasses: Unsettling the palate in the spaces between two continents. *European Journal of Life Writing* 6: 218–241. https://doi.org/10.4362/ejlw.6.213.

Tuck, Eve, and K. Wayne Yang. 2014a. R-words: Refusing research. In *Humanizing research: Decolonizing qualitative inquiry with youth and communities,* ed. D. Paris and M.T. Winn, 223–247. Thousand Oaks: SAGE.

———. 2014b. Unbecoming claims: Pedagogies of refusal in qualitative research. *Qualitative Inquiry* 20 (6): 811–818. https://doi.org/10.1177/1077800414530265.

CHAPTER 19

Intimacy: Torn

Abstract This chapter offers torn cartographies as a theoretical frame to conceptualize and engage with trans bodies, trans histories, and trans health research in Newfoundland. As impressions of postmodern fragmentation, torn cartographies trace the relational and shifting positions that trans women islanders live. By acknowledging the ruptured assemblage of archival absence, longing, and loss in relation to trans women's health, this chapter adds to the fields of emotional geographies and rural trans health studies.

Keywords Torn • Emotional geographies • Trans • Health • Fragmentation • Borderlands

When my lover passed away in late 2017, I grieved by spending time with the ocean. Both centered and unsettled by the crashing of waves—drawn into the instability of the harbour—I relied on the water to guide me, to help take the edge off my reality from which he had vanished. Like trying to measure the changing distance between wave troughs, adapting to everyday life without my darling next to me seemed hopeless. I wanted to drift just under the surface, feeling weightless for a moment. I wanted my ears to flood with water and then pop, forcing me to wake up from a nightmare. But everything was real.

I had been gutted like a fish. Sliced, cut, torn. Next to water, I was finding my way back home. Breathing in the salt, hearing the soft drones of

© The Author(s) 2018
S. Boon et al., *Autoethnography and Feminist Theory at the Water's Edge*, https://doi.org/10.1007/978-3-319-90829-8_19

waves churning, and sending my deepest, soul-aching love out to the sea, I promised him I would work twice as hard for the both of us. One night, the moon shone across the surface of the calm water in a long, silver streak like a rip from the dark horizon to the edge of the wharf where I stood. I imagined it as a rupture in time. If I dove into it, where would I end up? Could it pull me through to a better place?

Carved by oceanic, historical, hormonal, and surgical interventions, my life as a trans woman Newfoundlander might best be understood as torn. Situated within an emotional landscape of history, place, and sex, I envision the torn as a cartographic framework (Braidotti 2011) for creatively navigating the dissonance between Newfoundland's historical past and trans women's health in the present. A tool for pulling the self across place-based relations that shape trans lives, the torn rips its way beyond the corporeal limits of women like me and invites others into the ruptured geography (Brand 2001, 5)—the elsewhere (Rogowska-Stangret 2017) or "ecology of belonging" (Braidotti 2014, 167)—within which we, trans women islanders, live.

Who am I as a Newfoundland trans woman? How can I seek out or map where I belong as I yearn for trans history (Brand 2001)? How does not knowing my place in the historical past affect my health? I stand at a precipice that extends no longer, wishing to jump into the ocean to find room for living within the island's fishy trans past (see also Chap. 2). As if I am reading a genealogical record with frayed edges and missing pages, I recognize no traceable origin or roots (see also Chaps. 4 and 18). I accept that I must write the text I ache to know. As I grow torn, I question: How, or who, can I become without a history of trans women islanders?

While I cannot find archival traces of our lives, I use my imagination to feel less displaced (see Chaps. 2 and 16). Then I experience the ruptured materiality of my presence tearing through the archival fabric of island womanhood. As I push forward through torn cartographies, I write an opening—a split—to consider how trans experience changes what it means to 'do' womanhood (Butler 2004) in rural places. Trans women islanders are postmodern subjects, bodies in fragments (Eades 2017). Our subjectivities are shaped in spaces of hyphenation (Wah 2006). Thus, as impressions of embodied sociality (Connell 2009), and schemas out of historical erasure (Brand 2001) toward better-documented trans futures in Newfoundland, torn cartographies trace the relational and shifting positions that we live.

As I become-with, be-with, and live-with other women like me, I develop emotive and textured understandings of the mental and physical labour required for us to thrive at the water's edge. Through our entanglements, I come to know also a range of necessary choices trans women islanders make to survive. Theorizing torn cartographies is an act of my own mental labour as I work through notions of history and loss to contextualize my body and health as becoming-with others, both cis and trans islanders. Bound within an imagined community and by spatio-temporal shifts across and relations to sex, we become-together. We are skin to skin, we are torn. As such, the close and intimate intra-active (Barad 2007; Bettcher and Goulimari 2017) life narratives of trans women islanders open up possibilities for understanding linked politics of labour and health in rural places.

"Becoming-with," suggests Kate Wright, "offers a metaphysics grounded in connection" (2014, 278) whereby our relations to others, both human and more-than-human, are expressed through affective touches and textures (Vaccaro 2010). With and alongside others in liminal spaces of transition, trans women islanders engage in ruptured processes of becoming-with geographic, historical, and sexual spheres. Therefore, torn cartographies are sites and processes of erosion (see also Chap. 10). They tear and gnaw at the smooth and striated spaces (Deleuze and Guattari 1987) within which we survive.

Torn cartographies weave theory from texture, but unlike Sonja Boon's theory in/of/through stitches (see Chap. 13), the meaning of the torn is found in rips. An affective simulacrum of fragmentation, the torn is a space to map fractures, margins, splits, slashes, borderlands, and the troubles they create. Like Donna Haraway with her string figures, who seeks "a knotted analytical practice … [where] the tangles are necessary" (1994, 69), I recognize the torn as both an affective response to absence, and a transcorporeal (Alaimo 2010) becoming-with to understand the body in transition navigating frictional geographic and historical positions.

I call for others to embrace the torn. In so doing, we can engage together in a process of becoming-minoritarian (Deleuze and Guattari 1987), a practice of enfolding our selves to recognize—to live-with and be-with—a myriad of trans ontological positions. By investing emotional attention into the multiplex ways trans women's lives are lived, as well as the ways we understand our fragmented or eroded positions within the geographies of our home, each of us can know how it feels to be torn.

Most significantly, to become-with trans women islanders is to open up space for a touching methodological venture into our bodies and health (Thien 2012, 423). However, while forming affective relations to the study of trans health is necessary to contextualize the social underpinnings of trans matters in Newfoundland, I also argue that this process requires an intimate reflexivity from those who do not experience the labour of transition in this place. Our lives in the present become torn in relation to several missing pieces of the past: a lack of research, a lack of archival documents, and therefore a lack of representation (Namaste 2005). Displaced yet resilient, we long to know our place within the island's historical and physical landscapes.

Though intimately connected to the undocumented past, the torn is also a configuration for understanding our health in the future. Torn and fragmented approaches to trans health studies offer something critical to a tradition of Newfoundland scholarship: they unsettle topographies and gendered interrelations by which islanders have been carved and eroded for centuries, and they become reference points to both acknowledge and grieve over tattered and uncertain histories. In this moment, I move through temporal landscapes, a past-present-future becoming (simpkins 2017) with the torn. Surrounded by ruptures and tears, I am "half-in and half-out, coming and going, opening and closing: becoming" (Eades 2015, 232).

The torn has been most helpful to me as a tool to research and articulate suffering (Frank 2001). Across these pages, I burst with feeling. The weight of my heart leaks out like the light of the moon breaking the water's surface, but unlike that solar reflection, my life is dimly-lit. Here in this body, this geography (Rich 1994; Stryker 2008), the torn is a fold for grieving: first over archival invisibility and historical absence, but most powerfully and painfully over the loss of my wild lover, Dr. Yuvraj Gill, who passed over these earthly borderlands into the unknown much too soon.

I have poured a thousand briny questions into the ice-cold waters that surround my home, and I have allowed myself to be fragmented and undone as I hold on to our love. In the intimate spaces where memory and landscape overlap (Jones 2005), I fold back toward my time spent with Yuvraj and ache as I learn from the love we made, kneaded, and harboured. I feel him near the ocean and long to meet him there. In a dream, I see myself hitting the water and sinking, traveling soaking wet through a rough undertow and becoming tangled in a seine net. I am almost out of breath when he frees me. And although I begin to fade out, I am propelled to the surface and float in a pool of silver. He's here with me: it's alright now. I'm in pain, but it's the good kind. I am torn in his arms and I am bleeding theory. I am covered in cuts that will turn to silver scars.

By bringing critical and emotional attention to trans women's lives in Newfoundland, I ask each of us to consider the complex interplay between trans history, health, and belonging on this island we call home. A torn approach to rural trans health studies can help visualize currently hidden inflexures of the health, bodies and lives of trans women islanders. If, as Deborah Thien argues, "the emotional self or feeling subject is ever form-ing ... always becoming intelligible synchronously with places ... encoun-tered" (2012, 433), then becoming-with trans women Newfoundlanders is one way that others can begin to experience the push and pull of torn cartographies in sensuous and emotional geographies.

[DJ]

For Dr. Yuvraj Gill (1992–2017) who with his love has shown me new ways of studying trans health.

REFERENCES

Alaimo, Stacy. 2010. *Bodily natures: Science, environment, and the material self.* Bloomington: Indiana University Press.

Barad, Karen. 2007. *Meeting the universe halfway: Quantum physics and the entan-glement of matter and meaning.* Durham: Duke University Press.

Bettcher, Talia, and Pelagia Goulimari. 2017. Theorizing closeness: A trans femi-nist conversation. *Angelaki: Journal of the Theoretical Humanities* 22 (1): 49–60. https://doi.org/10.1080/0969725X.2017.1285608.

Braidotti, Rosi. 2011. *Nomadic subjects: Embodiment and sexual difference in con-temporary feminist theory.* 2nd ed. New York: Columbia University Press.

———. 2014. Writing as a nomadic subject. *Comparative Critical Studies* 11 (2–3): 163–184. https://doi.org/10.3366/ccs.2014.0122.

Brand, Dionne. 2001. *A map to the Door of No Return: Notes to belonging.* Toronto: Vintage Canada.

Butler, Judith. 2004. *Undoing gender.* New York and London: Routledge.

Connell, Raewyn. 2009. *Gender: In world perspective.* Cambridge: Polity.

Deleuze, Gilles, and Felix Guattari. 1987. *A thousand plateaus: Capitalism and schizophrenia.* Minneapolis: University of Minneapolis Press.

Eades, Quinn. 2015. *All the beginnings: A queer autobiography of the body.* North Melbourne: Tantanoola.

———. 2017. Transpoetics: Dialogically writing the queer and trans body in fragments. *Axon: Creative Explorations* 7 (2). http://axonjournal.com.au/issue-13/transpoetics.

Frank, Arthur. 2001. Can we research suffering? *Qualiative Health Research* 11 (3): 353–362. https://doi.org/10.1177/104973201129119154.

Haraway, Donna. 1994. A game of cat's cradle: Science studies, feminist theory, cultural studies. *Configurations* 2 (1): 59–71. https://doi.org/10.1353/con.1994.0009.

Jones, Owain. 2005. An ecology of emotion, memory, self and landscape. In *Emotional geographies*, ed. Joyce Davidson, Liz Bondi, and Mick Smith, 205–218. Aldershot: Ashgate.

Namaste, Viviane. 2005. *Sex change, social change: Reflections on identity, institutions and imperialism.* Toronto: Women's Press.

Rich, Adrienne. 1994. Notes towards a politics of location. In *Blood, bread, and poetry: Selected prose, 1979–1985,* 210–231. New York: Norton.

Rogowska-Stangret, Monika. 2017. Corpor(e)al cartographies of new materialism. *The Minnesota Review* 88: 56–68. https://doi.org/10.1215/0026 5667-3787390.

simpkins, reese. 2017. Temporal flesh, material becomings. *Somatechnics* 7 (1): 124–141. https://doi.org/10.3366/soma.2017.0209.

Stryker, Susan. 2008. Dungeon intimacies: The poetics of transsexual sadomasochism. *Parallax* 14 (1): 36–47. https://doi.org/10.1080/135346407017 81362.

Thien, Deborah. 2012. Well beings: Placing emotion in rural, gender, and health research. In *Rural Women's Health*, ed. Beverly Leipert, Belinda Leach, and Wilfreda Thurston, 423–440. Toronto: University of Toronto Press.

Vaccaro, Jeanne. 2010. Felt matters. *Women & Performance: A Journal of Feminist Theory* 20 (3): 253–266. https://doi.org/10.1080/0740770X.2010.529245.

Wah, Fred. 2006. *Diamond grill.* Edmonton: NeWest Press.

Wright, Kate. 2014. Becoming-with: Living lexicon for the environmental humanities. *Environmental Humanities* 5: 277–281. https://doi.org/10.1215/22011919-3615514.

CHAPTER 20

Belongings: Stumble

Abstract Drawing on the literature of sensuous geographies as well as on the work of Sara Ahmed and Rosemarie Garland Thomson, this chapter considers what it means to stumble, and what stumbling—a state of suspension, a liminal space between vertical and horizontal—might reveal about the relationships between bodies and the land on which they live, and from there, what it might tell us about belonging.

Keywords Sensuous geography • Misfitting • Stumble • Embodiment

If the body is, as Adrienne Rich has argued, "the geography closest in" (1994, 212), then what might this body tell me about the physical geographies of this place I call home? What happens when these two geographies—internal and external—encounter one another?

Here, on the edge of the North Atlantic, the land and I meet. My footfall wears a path in the grass, joining the stories of all those who have walked these desire lines before me. I am tentative, my feet feeling for security. Around me on Newfoundland's East Coast Trail, others move faster, bodies and land worlding together, relationships between internal and external geographies well honed. Some even run, their steps secure, ponytails bounding. But I pause regularly. I say it's to enjoy the view. And perhaps it is. But mostly it's because I need to find my body, to locate my toes, to feel the earth and rock beneath my feet. I stumble. I can't find my footing. Geography betrays me. The land, it seems, resists.

© The Author(s) 2018
S. Boon et al., *Autoethnography and Feminist Theory at the Water's Edge*, https://doi.org/10.1007/978-3-319-90829-8_20

Place, as Steven Feld has observed, is sensuous (2005, 179; see also Cresswell 2010; Jones 2004); it is, as Tim Cresswell writes, "a way of seeing, knowing and understanding the world" (2004, 11; see also Rodaway 1994, 31 and Chap. 17, earlier in this volume). There is a fleshiness to geography. It stands to reason then that migration, the act of moving from one place to another, involves a "spatial reconfiguration of an embodied self" (Ahmed 2000, 90). Internal and external geography must come to know one another anew, body and world learning each other's rhythms, moods, and feelings. Mapping is how I work through my belonging, but there is much my body cannot map here (see also Chap. 11).

The ocean encroaches; it rushes in, eats away, makes things unstable, unsettled, unpredictable. On islands, land ends. And this is what my prairie-raised body has not yet come to understand. What is a cliff? How do I navigate it? The geography within does not comprehend these limits, these boundaries. I don't trust this land and in turn, I am not certain that it trusts me.

Where do we locate ourselves if our bodies and our spaces don't match up, if our internal and external geographies aren't in sync, if we cannot find a common rhythm? After a decade on this island, I am still buffeted by winds, uprooted, uncertain. The water troubles me; I do not have faith in it. Cliff edges haunt my dreams. I find myself clinging to anything that seems fixed, seeking security in a bending twig. My toes catch in the tangled roots of a tuckamore. My shoulders tense, tighten. My breath shortens, gasps. I can't feel my body anymore. Geography has unmade me, disassembled me. How do I map this place, and how has it mapped me? Looking out at the rolling ocean, I long for the solidity of the endless wheat fields of my childhood.

My stumbles remind me that I am out of place. I do not fit here, and perhaps, then, my corporeal uncertainty must be read as stigmata, the mark of one who has not worlded with this place. I am a stranger here (Ahmed 2000). This landscape does not sustain me, and I, in turn, have not learned how to sustain it. But Rosemarie Garland Thomson reminds me that misfitting is about entanglement; it is about process and encounter: "A misfit occurs when the environment does not sustain the shape and function of the body that enters it" (2011, 594). Perhaps, then, Newfoundland and I are not a good fit for one another. Perhaps my frequent stumbles are a material evocation of my social status, a continual reminder that identity, Newfoundland-style, does not include me.

Stumble. To fall. Involuntary. To jostle against. To stumble is to exist in a state of suspension, a liminal space between vertical and horizontal. A stumble is a relationship between the body and the land it is attempting to navigate. Time stops. I don't know where I will land.

And yet, after a decade here, the lines have softened. I'm no longer fully from away, but nor am I from here. I am from somewhere in between, "an act of kneading" (Anzaldúa 2012, 103). And in this space, my stumbles take on a new cast. Stumble: the *entredeux* (Cixous and Calle-Gruber 1997) of my belonging along the frayed edges of a map (Wah 2006), the Door of No Return (Brand 2001). My islandness is an islandness on the edges, an island-ness of stumbling, misfitting, otherness where the water meets the land.

[SB]

References

Ahmed, Sara. 2000. *Strange encounters: Embodied others in post-coloniality.* London and New York: Routledge.

Anzaldúa, Gloria. 2012. *Borderlands/la frontera: The new mestiza.* 4th ed. San Francisco: Aunt Lute.

Brand, Dionne. 2001. *A map to the Door of No Return: Notes to belonging.* Toronto: Vintage Canada.

Cixous, Hélène, and Mireille Calle-Gruber. 1997. *Hélène Cixous, Rootprints: Memory and life writing.* Trans. by Eric Prenowitz. London and New York: Routledge.

Cresswell, Tim. 2004. *Place: A short introduction.* Malden: Blackwell.

———. 2010. Towards a politics of mobility. *Environment and Planning D: Society and Space* 28: 17–31. https://doi.org/10.1068/d11407.

Feld, Steven. 2005. Places sensed, senses placed: Toward a sensuous epistemology of environments. In *Empire of the senses: The sensual culture reader,* ed. David Howes, 179–191. Oxford and New York: Berg.

Garland Thomson, Rosemarie. 2011. Misfits: A feminist materialist disability concept. *Hypatia* 26 (3): 591–609.

Jones, Owain. 2004. An ecology of emotion, self, memory and landscape. In *Emotional geographies,* ed. Joyce Davidson, Liz Bondi, and Mick Smith, 205–218. Aldershot: Ashgate.

Rich, Adrienne. 1994. Notes towards a politics of location (1984). In *Blood, bread, and poetry: Selected prose, 1979–1985,* 210–231. New York: Norton.

Rodaway, Paul. 1994. *Sensuous geographies: Body, sense, and place.* London and New York: Blackwell.

Wah, Fred. 2006. *Diamond grill.* Edmonton: NeWest Press.

Index

© The Author(s) 2018   139
S. Boon et al., *Autoethnography and Feminist Theory at the Water's Edge*, https://doi.org/10.1007/978-3-319-90829-8

Lightning Source UK Ltd.
Milton Keynes UK
UKHW020221261119
354225UK00007B/464/P